MILKY WAYS
and
FIREFLIES

words of wonder for tattered souls

K. WILLIAM KAUTZ

outskirts press

Milky Ways and Fireflies
words of wonder for tattered souls
All Rights Reserved.
Copyright © 2023 K. William Kautz
v2.0

The opinions expressed in this manuscript are solely the opinions of the author and do not represent the opinions or thoughts of the publisher. The author has represented and warranted full ownership and/or legal right to publish all the materials in this book.

This book may not be reproduced, transmitted, or stored in whole or in part by any means, including graphic, electronic, or mechanical without the express written consent of the publisher except in the case of brief quotations embodied in critical articles and reviews.

Outskirts Press, Inc.
http://www.outskirtspress.com

Paperback ISBN: 978-1-9772-6168-7
Hardback ISBN: 978-1-9772-6228-8

Cover Design by K. William Kautz
Cover Photography © 2023 Simanta V. Mahanta. All rights reserved - used with permission.

Outskirts Press and the "OP" logo are trademarks belonging to Outskirts Press, Inc.

PRINTED IN THE UNITED STATES OF AMERICA

Table of Contents

Foreword i

PART ONE - The Intersection of Pain and Purpose
1 Crawling through the Breaches 3
2 Milky Ways and Fireflies 10
3 The Cradle of Art and Science 14
4 The Lenses of our Lives 18
5 Nathaniel 25
6 Still Standing 28
7 The Sacrament of Grief 34
8 Every Square Inch 38
9 Live Everything 42
10 Maligne Lake 46
11 Liquid Love and Loneliness 50

PART TWO - Graceland
12 Love Beneath the Veil 57
13 Someone I Love 62
14 Facing the Deep 65

15 Courage 69
16 Wearing Masks 73
17 The Splendor of our Inadequacies 77
18 Dying to Live 81

PART THREE - Betrayals and Other Blessings
19 Surviving the Flying Monkeys 87
20 The Ugly Silence 92
21 Their Finest Hour 95
22 Love Letter to a Scapegoat 99
23 The Intifada of the Soul 103
24 Forgiven 107
25 Epiphanies 111
26 Finding Home 114

PART FOUR - Life After Loss
27 Awakening 119
28 Penniless Wealth and Perilous Joy 125
29 Treasures 130
30 Consider the Birds 134
31 Beautiful 138
32 Beacons in a Darkened Space 141
33 Mars Hill Revisited 145
34 Keeping Vigil 149
35 The Rude Vigor of Truth 155
36 Shaking the Dust 160
37 Unseen Things 164
38 Grace and Power 170
39 Making Joy 174
40 Rising from the Dead 178

Foreword

This book began as a series of small essays posted on social media. After the deaths of two of my children, I began to think and write about those fears and passions we all have in common - no matter what our backgrounds. When one of my posts went viral, I suddenly had a large audience of people from far away places. There was one response that I kept receiving from my readers. They would tell me how inadequate they felt about expressing their own yearnings and they were grateful that someone was doing it for them. There is something about giving voice to the deepest longings of the human heart that is healing to both the writer and the reader. This is what I've attempted in these pages.

I picked the subtitle because it seems to fit everyone. A tattered soul describes all the walking wounded who make up the human race. They are liberals and conservatives, women and men - people of all different races, nationalities and ages. Some are artists and dreamers who might be spiritually unaffiliated while others are conservative folk who want everything to be neat and tidy. Some are introverts - energized by solitude and depleted by people. Others are the extroverts who pity them. Some are sweet, feral seekers who could never be spiritually domesticated. Others might be the adherents of fundamentalism. I just wanted to offer grace to anyone who has ever longed for something just beyond their reach…

PART ONE – THE INTERSECTION OF PAIN AND PURPOSE

1

Crawling through the Breaches

This is a book about becoming. It is about embracing our inadequacies, letting go of false securities, turning wounds to wisdom and finding ourselves in the process. It is a book about epiphanies and ah-ha moments when our souls are transformed and everything becomes new again. Sometimes the profound complexities of life and the crucible of trauma and loss can jump-start our spiritual formation so that things like character, authenticity and integrity become more important to us than ever before. It often happens when we are sent to a land of brokenness and in that lonely place, our eyes are mysteriously opened and wonders are revealed.

Before the process begins, there is a deadly comfort. It forbids growth. It denies truth. It is blind to the suffering of others. We wander aimlessly without direction in a life devoid of meaning and we find ourselves at times, infatuated by the mundane. We collect stuff and store-up treasures that are easily consumed by moth and rust. Others might envy us but inside our hearts there is an emptiness that yearns to be filled with things unknown.

And then something happens. It might be a tragedy. It might be an experience that shakes us to the core. It might be something so beautiful and full of splendor that our eyes can no longer focus on former things. Suddenly, we find ourselves on a 'road less traveled' and nothing will ever be the same again.

It always seems to begin with humility. It is that imperishable stuff of eternity. Every good thing starts there and nothing truly transformative ever happens without it. When we see it in another soul, there is something magical about it. We find ourselves wondering what kind of power enables it and we are mesmerized by its beauty.

My earliest encounter with it occurred when I was five years old. My family was having dinner together one evening when I accidentally dropped my napkin on the floor. I went under the table to fetch it but my dad thought I was being mischievous. He called my name sternly and I got scared and banged my head against the underside of the table. As I crawled back into my chair, I exclaimed, "Ow! I was just getting my napkin!" A sudden look of sorrow came over my dad's face.

Then he apologized.

I started to cry - not because my head hurt, but because the moment was so touching. I wouldn't have been able to express it then, but I was moved by it. I guess I was a sensitive kid. At the time, my dad seemed so powerful to me. He didn't have to humble himself. He held all the cards. No one was making him do it yet he did it anyway. It seems like a small thing now, but it wasn't small then, and I obviously never forgot it.

I often wonder why some people can acknowledge a mistake so easily while others find it nearly impossible. It's such a mystery. But I've never met anyone who hates seeing humility in another person. We all feel safe around someone who admits a failure. In fact, we long to be in community with such people. It's as if we instinctively know that perfection isn't possible but those who can be real and honest and transparent make us feel cherished and secure.

Put those thoughts on a back burner for a few minutes. I'll return to them shortly but first, I want to tell you about a collision I saw in Nicaragua involving an angry American teenager. It wasn't a car collision. It was a collision of two worlds. She was fifteen years old and a sophomore in a Midwestern high school. She volunteered to go to Nicaragua with a group of other kids who wanted to get out of town and see the world. She imagined volcanos and lakes and 16th century Spanish architecture. Her parents paid for the trip. She knew she'd also be doing some volunteer work but she had absolutely no idea what she was getting herself into.

Like many teenage girls, she was focused on clothes, boys, cell phones and what other people thought of her. She obviously came from affluence. She was the quintessential product of her culture. I caught my first glimpse of what might be the mischievousness of God when she began her complaints. She didn't like the heat and she seemed unaccustomed to work. Her face displayed one of those pursed-lip, sour-puss, teenage rebel expressions that we've all seen before. She also didn't want to paint a dilapidated school that was parked in the middle of a garbage dump. The children who lived in the dump attended the school which only served grades K-3. The toilets were broken. The paint was peeling. The cement walls were cracked. We arrived early in the morning before all the little students but we caught glimpses of the pitiful shacks they called 'home.' Emaciated dogs wandered the grounds and the stench of garbage was everywhere.

A stunned silence hung in the air as each of us tried to absorb it all. No one felt like talking.

I've been curious about human subjectivity - and how to get around it, ever since I was a kid. We all tend to think of ourselves as 'objective' and those who disagree with us as 'subjective'. We think, "If only people would see what I see, they would agree that I'm right." I can't help laughing at myself as I even write those words. But we all do it. We all convince ourselves of our own objectivity - which only proves how subjective we really are.

Later, when I was in law school, I learned of a legal theory called 'Critical Legal Studies.' It basically says that objectivity is impossible because we all view life through the lenses of our own experiences. We all come from some place and our orientation distorts reality so much that truth is indeterminate. It is a paralyzing theory that is devoid of hope. When I first encountered it, I thought its diagnosis of the human condition was brilliant but its pessimism bothered me. There is a term used to describe those who hold to such theories. It is 'epistemological humility.' It's just a fancy phrase for those who recognize the fundamental problem facing us all.

So... Is there really no way out? Is there no way to transcend our blinding biases? What has to happen before we are each willing to strip ourselves of everything that holds us back?

There's another term I learned long ago. It's not academically fancy. But it contains more depth than anything I know. It is, *a broken and contrite heart.*

Now let's go back to the dump where two worlds are colliding. A few minutes after we arrived at the school, a stream of children appeared. They were dressed in sparkling white shirts and dark blue skirts or pants. We all viewed the spectacle with awe and wondered, 'How did their moms get those shirts so clean while living in a filthy dump?'

The expression on the face of the teenage girl changed immediately. The little kids with the sparkling white shirts marched into her world with joy. It was like two galaxies colliding. Nothing would ever be the same again. The children clamored around her like she was a rock star. They longed for her embrace. These colliding worlds didn't speak the same language but something transformational was happening. Sometimes language isn't necessary. Sometimes God shows us ourselves without a single word. Sometimes he just spits into the dirt and rubs the mud into our eyes until the scales fall off and everything becomes new again. Sometimes he does it in the most cunning ways.

I watched that teenage girl for a week. I saw her rebellion melt away. I saw a self-absorbed child become a beautiful young woman. I saw her *want* to work. In the oppressive heat. With joy. At one point, some school girls from the dump climbed into her lap and she just seemed to collapse into a new life - like one surrendering everything she once held dear. It was as if she was letting go of the shallow and the mundane so she could grab onto something deep.

After seeing this, I found myself praying to someone who might have brought all of this about: "What just happened? She came here oblivious to your plans. She was completely defenseless against the power of your will. You were like a cunning trickster with sneaky intent. You never preached. You never coerced. You knew what she needed. You knew how to love her deeply. You knew she would never be happy until she was taken out of her world and shown another. What an ingenious twist of the narrative - a glimpse into hell gave her a vision of heaven."

So here's the thing: Even a 5-year old child can see the beauty of humility. Even a child can see how relationships can be transformed by it. When my dad, who seemed so powerful to me, took it upon himself to say that he was sorry, the impact of that apology made a lasting impression on me. It made me want to live among the broken and contrite because I knew that was the only place I would ever be safe.

But the social jungle tells us that humility is weakness and it equates surrender with defeat. It tells us to ward off attacks by hiding our wounds. There is something so counterintuitive about the idea that surrender and humility might actually lead to victory and power instead. We resist acknowledging our inadequacies even though that is the very thing that will enable us to get past our blinding biases. It is so easy to cherish our subjectivities when a deep sense of vulnerability causes us to build castle walls and a moat around us so that no foreign thought can ever disturb our ease. Anyone who blows a hole in our defenses must be an enemy, right? But what if the canons of eternity are trained against our walls so that we can escape the prisons we've built for ourselves? What if there is far more joy and deep, redeeming truths outside of our walls and the only way to get to them is to crawl through the breaches ...and surrender?

2

Milky Ways and Fireflies

Leaving the prisons we've built for ourselves is a first step. Now we need the innocence of a child whose mind is still open, curious and pliable. Whenever I want to retrieve the wonder of my childhood, I go outside on a starry night and stand in awe of it all. I love the way the universe dwarfs us without humiliating us. It teaches us not to think too highly of ourselves and at the same time, we are invited to participate in its magnificence because we have the capacity to fall in love with integrity, compassion, mercy, grace and truth and be transformed by those things.

The best time to see the universe is when everyone else is sleeping. There is less ambient light and nothing to distract us. Some people don't like getting out of a cozy bed in the middle of the night, but I do because something magical usually happens. My second floor window overlooks a field. Beyond that is a mountain and above it all is a thing of wonder. In the wintertime, it's so cold outside that the moisture in the air freezes and falls to the ground leaving the night sky clear and crisp as the Milky Way stretches from north to south. In the summertime, there are dozens of fireflies in the field beside my house and they dance beneath the canopy of space in a universe of their own. I like to think about how a little bug with a lantern inside can look the same size as a massive star - a million light-years from my home.

An elementary school teacher once told me that the greatest thing we can cultivate in a child is a sense of wonder. I like that. But... most of the children I know already have a sense of wonder because they're seeing things for the first time. It's the adults who have lost the ability to be amazed by the glories that surround us. We are the ones who need to get out of bed in the middle of the night to watch the fireflies perform beneath the Milky Way and just stand in awe of everything that is.

When I was about ten years old, my dad caught me laying on my bed - staring at the ceiling on a beautiful sunny day. He said, "What are you doing? It's a perfect day and all the kids are playing ball!" I replied, "I'm thinking." He shook his head and politely closed the door. I guess I'm a little odd but I was puzzled by the impossibility of everything. I couldn't understand how a single thing could be. Either the stuff of the universe always existed without beginning or something began out of nothing. Both propositions boggle the mind.

Lately I've been thinking that spirituality is about the movement from ignorance to unknowing to wonder. Those are the three states of being that life takes us through - whether we are willing to go or not.

Ignorance is the desire to remain uninformed because certain truths disturb us and we prefer not to be challenged.

We have all run away from honest scholastic inquiry at various times in our lives because it's just easier to see everything in black and white terms and it's terrifying to discover that life can be more complicated than we ever wanted it to be. Usually the desire to remain ignorant is shattered when tragedy strikes or something painful happens to us and we are forced out of our comfort zones to look for things that never interested us before.

Unknowing is an awesome stage. It's also not very fun. But the important thing is that it's the beginning of integrity. It is that scary process of letting go of former things that brought us false comfort and damaged us and kept us from growing. My dad once told me about some art students he was teaching. A few of them had painted for years before coming to his class. They were self-taught and their amateur paintings were unimpressive. Other students had never picked up a paint brush in their lives. One guy had a heart condition so his doctor told him to find a relaxing hobby. A few days later he showed up at my dad's class without any experience at all. My dad told me it was so much easier to teach the guy with the heart condition because he didn't have to unlearn all the bad habits that defined the other students. Those bad habits prevented any kind of meaningful growth. But then the guy with the heart condition began producing artwork that put everyone else to shame. Suddenly the other students realized their need for a teacher and began the painful process of unknowing the nonsense they had taught themselves. Such are the moments that change everything.

Wonder is that deeply spiritual place we come to when we earnestly want to know the truth and are willing to give up anything to find it but... it's unavailable to us because some things are just too mysterious to grasp. For some reason though, we also discover it to be a place of joy because we realize it's ok to not have all the answers and to accept the brokenness we felt when we first came face to face with our own inadequacies. Richard Rohr once wrote, *"Those who know God well - mystics, hermits, prayerful people, those who risk everything to find God - always meet a lover, not a dictator."*[1] This is what we find in that place of brokenness and wonder. Suddenly, it's ok to place our lives in the hands of a tender God and begin a journey of faith. Darkness is no longer a place of terror. It is a place of Milky Way wonder and we start to see those around us as fellow pilgrims struggling with the same humbling questions. Grace begins to flow out of us then and the intolerance that once defined us no longer has a place in our lives. When we see another creature struggling under the weight of oppression or infirmity or hopelessness, our capacity to love grows even stronger and we become like fireflies with little lanterns inside us - dancing beneath the canopy of incomprehensible space.

---

[1] Richard Rohr, *Everything Belongs: The Gift of Contemplative Prayer* (Holland, Ohio: Dreamscape Media LLC, 2003)

3

The Cradle of Art and Science

Spiritual journeys can be embarrassing things. In my early years I was defined by a presumptuous confidence. When I saw the same trait in other people, I didn't like it and decided to change. I hadn't yet encountered anything that humbled me. But I knew I didn't want to be an arrogant man.

Then life happened and I was left asking questions that couldn't be answered. Many years later, I found two quotes. The first has been attributed to Mark Twain. The second is from Albert Einstein. Both seem true but Twain's is more cynical than I prefer, while Einstein's is filled with joy...

Mark Twain: *"Education is the path from cocky ignorance to miserable uncertainty."*

Albert Einstein: *"The most beautiful experience we can have is the mysterious. It is the fundamental emotion which stands at the cradle of true art and true science. Whoever does not know it and can no longer wonder, no longer marvel, is as good as dead and his eyes are dimmed."*[2]

These two quotes made me think about the difference between cynicism and skepticism. Cynicism paralyses us. Skepticism only asks us to question our biases. Cynicism is like a grumpy teenager who says, "Everything is stupid." Skepticism invites us to move beyond ourselves and challenge our untested assumptions. It's healthy to be skeptical about our subjectivity but cynicism destroys our spirits until we can no longer believe in anything.

Recently I discovered a study about the nature of liberalism and conservatism and I became fascinated by how they affect our spiritual development. The author of the study suggested that societies need both kinds of thinking.

Conservatives tend to prioritize order and predictability and are less comfortable with uncertainty. Liberals don't mind ambiguity and are better at understanding subtle nuances. Conservatives excel at organizing things and prefer everything to be tidy. Liberals are creative and don't mind a little chaos.

The weakness of the liberal mind is that it tends to show compassion without holding someone accountable for a mistake. Love without discipline will often produce mediocrity and failure.

The weakness of the conservative mind is that it wants so badly to bring order to chaos, that it sometimes chooses overly simplistic "answers" to difficult questions. For this reason, conservatives need to guard themselves from becoming like Pharisees - theological fundamentalists who "neglected

---

[2] Albert Einstein, *The World As I See It* (CreateSpace Independent Publishing Platform, 2014)

the weightier matters of justice and mercy."[3]

I was recently reunited with some old high school friends and was struck by how little they had changed in nearly fifty years. Their minds were gifted at regurgitating memorized orthodoxies but when it came to examining uncomfortable complexities they would run away in fear. As a result, they are the same people they were when we were teenagers. The moment we think we have everything figured out, we destroy our ability to grow.

When Moses encountered God in a burning bush he asked, "Who are you? What is your name?" God replied, *"I am who I am."*[4] It was as if Moses was being told, "Don't even presume to figure me out. My ways aren't your ways. Just take off your shoes on this holy ground. You are in the presence of the incomprehensible."

There is something so beautiful and holy about the mysterious. We don't need to understand it all in order to yearn for it. Holiness isn't just perfection. It's baffling too. It is something so far beyond us that we must either flee with our anger, our cowardice, and our arrogance ...or crumble to the ground in humility and awe. There is no place for hubris in the cradle of art and science.

This is why an open mind might not be the evil thing that some presume it to be. It isn't bothered by the mysterious because it glories in the wonder of it all. In fact, such a mind might even be cultivated by a baffling God. Why? Because the alternative is orthodoxy without humility, law without grace, and religion without mercy. When Paul of Tarsus looked back

---

3   Matthew 23:23,24
4   Exodus 3:14

at his former Pharisaism, he called it a pile of dung. There is nothing like encountering a blinding light that stops a person dead in his tracks and forces him to rethink all of his previous assumptions. The cradle of art and science is a place of glorious terror and unspeakable joy. It compels us to get over ourselves and at the same time, comforts us with a baffling truth: there is no wilder paradox and no safer place to be than in the presence of an incomprehensible love - emptied of everything and laying helpless in a cradle of mystery and straw.

4

The Lenses of our Lives

This is a story of redemption. I know that word can mean different things to different people but sometimes redemption shows itself in strange places. Sometimes a person's pain can be redeemed. Sometimes the anguish we're carrying might actually be the very thing that opens our eyes to something disarming and unexpected and transformational.

When my son died in an avalanche, he was 25 years old. Justin was healthy, happy, loving and mature. We had a camaraderie that I valued a lot. Shortly before he died, he sent me an email. In it he wrote, "Dad, you're the most honorable man I know. Thank you for teaching me how to love." Those are the words that a parent longs to hear and so when the news came of his loss, I was devastated.

I think I probably grieved in the usual way during the next two or three years. There was nothing exceptional about it. I was basically an emotional basket-case during the first year and gradually, over time, my mind adjusted to the 'new normal' even while that big gaping hole remained in my soul.

Then one day, I realized that I wasn't accomplishing anything of value. I was focused only on my losses. It was like I was viewing my pain through a camera with a zoom lens attached to it. I couldn't see peripheral things. I think it's healthy for a grieving person to focus on a loss. But there comes a time when we're ready to take off the zoom lens and begin viewing life through a wide-angle lens because redemption is often found hiding in the peripheries where no one thinks to look.

But... how do we do that? How do we begin searching for something that we've never experienced before – especially when we don't even know what it is?

Something told me that I needed to find people who had suffered more than me. So one day I sat in front of my computer and began googling things. I didn't know where to start and I forget how my search began but at the end of several hours I found myself watching a video of a little girl living in a garbage dump in Latin America. The place was called 'La Chureca' and there were hundreds of kids in that dump. I had never been to Latin America but when I saw that little girl, a mysterious feeling came over me that just said, "Go."

Ordinarily, I'm not the kind of person who says, "God told me this, or God told me that." There have been so many kooky people saying so many kooky things in the name of God and I just didn't want to be one of them. But when the word "Go" began reverberating in my soul, I recalled the day after Justin died. I remembered sitting on my bedroom floor with my face in the carpet, sobbing my heart out, and another mysterious feeling came over me then as if I was being told,

"This isn't an accident, Will. I am doing something. Trust me in the darkness."

So after reading about that garbage dump, I bought a ticket, got on a plane and headed to a place that travel agencies never tell you about. As soon as I arrived, I knew my life would never be the same.

Sometimes we encounter things that profoundly change our outlook on life and when it happens, it doesn't matter that former joys have lost their allure or that our foundations have been shaken. All we know is that the walls we've built around ourselves have crumbled into dust. Somehow, our unsatisfied yearnings no longer throb inside us and something restorative is taking place deep inside us.

Sitting on the outskirts of Managua, the dump has been called one of the most wretched places on earth. A few thousand people call it 'home.' They sift through the rubbish for food to eat or things to sell. The children begin their careers early. You can see them with their sticks – poking and prodding the soil for plastics or metal or something of value. Girls as young as nine years old prostitute themselves to the garbage truck drivers in exchange for the first pick from the truck.

This is a world where violence and innocence live side by side and where a young girl's best protection against a sexual predator is an emaciated body. The poverty is relentless. The shame is merciless. Disease pocks the scalps of tiny little heads. But despite all the danger, the place is strangely disarming. How can we poke our lives into such a world without lowering our guard? What is the point of my fortress when a daddyless girl wants to play with me? Brick and mortar melt like wax in the warmth of her smile and the glow of her eyes.

It's like falling in love with grace itself and I found myself not wanting to leave that miserable place.

Maybe I was nuts. Maybe I contracted a strange disorder. Maybe the heat got to me. Maybe I hadn't felt so alive in decades. Maybe I had to be emptied before I could ever be filled…

I have a faith. The spiritual tradition that I was raised in isn't very healthy these days and I've become completely disillusioned with it. But I never stopped believing in the goodness and grace of God. So I began praying that I could adopt one of those kids from Nicaragua. It was an impossible prayer and I knew it. The Nicaraguan government doesn't allow Americans to adopt anyone. I was also a single male who wasn't getting any younger and no agency would ever allow me to adopt a little girl anyway. But I prayed that prayer because I thought maybe God is the God of the impossible and I was crazy enough to believe anything could happen.

I eventually had to fly home but on my third trip to Nicaragua, something unexpected happened…

I had made arrangements with a Nicaraguan woman named Diana to translate for me. I was learning Spanish but… Es difícil porque mi cerebro está viejo y decrépito. So Diana was a life saver.

As soon as I arrived at the airport, Diana began telling me about her kid sister Jenny. Diana was one of those super-organized women who wanted to plan my itinerary by the hour - months in advance. I was the free-spirited artist who just wanted to go with the flow and Jenny, well… Jenny was a wreck. Her dad had died when she was two years old. The family lost everything. She spent her childhood in a third world hell. She had slept on floors as a child, gone days without food, suffered various indignities, developed an anxiety disorder with debilitating panic attacks and an extra dose of depression on the side. Diana wanted Jenny to just pick herself up and earn some money for the family but Jenny was having a tough time of it. She was 25 years old when I met her – the same age as Justin when I lost him.

The good news is that Jenny was very creative. She wanted to be a photographer but she had no camera – just a cheap cell phone that took pictures. She also had the disorganized personality of an artist. She didn't mind chaos in the bedroom she shared with her sister and that drove Diana absolutely nuts. It was an amusing spectacle to watch.

So one evening I took Diana and Jenny and their mom out to dinner. When we were on our way to the restaurant, Jenny began to talk. She said, "My family doesn't want me to say this but I've been having problems. I have panic attacks and depression and I don't know how to fix myself." Those few words almost made me cry. Not because they were sad, but because I wasn't used to the beauty of her honesty. Most people can't do what Jenny did. She was open and transparent and she had no interest in cultivating a fake veneer of perfection.

When we arrived at the restaurant, she took out her cell phone and showed me her photos. I was impressed. They weren't just pretty pictures. I could tell that she had an eye for composition and light and she also had one other thing that brought life to her work. She had a heart for vulnerable people. The more I listened to her, the more I saw how intelligent and analytical she was. By the end of the evening, I was in awe.

Sadly, after ten days, I had to fly home. Jenny surprised Diana by waking up at 5:30 in the morning to go to the airport with me. Ordinarily, Jenny was too depressed to get out of bed before noon. Some days she didn't get out of bed at all. So... Diana couldn't believe her eyes when her sister accompanied us to the airport. When we were there, I could tell that Jenny wanted to ask me something. But she didn't. So I got on the plane and flew home.

Once back in Vermont, I received an email. It was from Jenny. She wrote… "I have an unusual question for you. All my life, all I ever wanted was a dad. I never cared about toys. I just wanted a dad to spend time with me and encourage me and protect me. Would you be my dad? Would you help me to believe in myself? Would you help me overcome my problems?" My heart melted. I realized immediately that my impossible prayer was answered and that her humble cry for help would begin one of the sweetest chapters of my life.

After telling Jenny how honored I was to be her dad, I sent her a camera with lenses and a computer too. Then I asked her if there was a school in Managua where she could learn photography. She told me about a photo academy run by the French government as part of a cultural exchange effort. We enrolled her. A few weeks later, I received an email from a psychiatrist in Managua who had been helping Jenny for free. She said, "I cannot believe the transformation that is happening to your daughter! She wakes up early each morning, goes to school, does her homework, and teaches herself photo editing online." A few months later, Jenny's professor said, "Your daughter is a frickin' genius!"

Jenny graduated at the top of her class and has since

established a name for herself in her field. When she visits me in the US, she is full of joy. She loves being in my workshop as I sculpt and paint. She says, "Teach me Dad! I want to learn!" When we go places, she brags about me to others. She says, "My dad is an honorable man!" I can't begin to express the joy this brings after years of mourning. She tells everyone our story. People cry. In some mysterious way, the most heart-breaking events of our lives gave birth to the most beautiful events of our lives.

So I'll end here with perhaps the only words that really matter because… there are mysteries also hidden in the peripheries of your life. They are waiting to be found with a wide-angle lens while you mourn your losses and bear your pain. There is also a voice calling from the deep and offering to redeem that pain with words that are disarming, unexpected and transformational:

> "This isn't an accident"
> "I'm doing something."
> "Trust me in the darkness."
> "Go."

5

Nathaniel

I have lost two sons. The first died in the snows of Wyoming, the second took his own life. Nathaniel had struggled with depression ever since he was in his early teens. He was 33 years old when he died. I'm not writing this because I want sympathy. I'm looking for something else.

I know this might seem strange to those who never raised a child with mental illness, but I mourned Nate's loss for two decades before he died. There had been so many suicide attempts, so many bloody traumas, and so many failed efforts to get him help, that I had already resigned myself to the inevitable.

At first, his depression was accompanied by rebellion but after all the damage had been done, Nate came to me one day and said, "I'm sorry, Dad. I've dug such a deep hole for myself and I don't know how I can ever recover." He was contrite and endearing and we were able to talk about deeper things even though the brooding remained. Then, he met a young woman and got married. A baby was born and they were both very happy. Baby Max looked just like Nate and my son suddenly seemed full of hope.

But the joy lasted only a month. One night, Max went to sleep and never woke up. When they found the baby, his lips were blue and there was nothing anyone could do. The baby was only 38 days old and Nate fell into his final bout of depression.

So here's what I really want to say about mental illness...

If a child is born with a hole in her heart, everyone in our society would respond the same way. We would all ask, "Is there something we can do?" No one would ever wag his head at the child or the parents and say, "You must have done something wrong." We would all offer sympathy rather than condemnation. But when a child is born with a chemical imbalance or a genetic predisposition towards depression, that child and his/her parents can look forward to a lifetime of shame and blame from a society that is truly clueless about the nature of the problem.

What we need to understand is that the brain is just an organ. It may be the most complicated organ in the body, but it is still just a mass of biological stuff that is susceptible to disease just like a liver or a lung or a pancreas. The fact that our culture offers sympathy to a patient with a damaged heart but wags its collective head at a patient with a damaged brain suggests that we really never left the dark ages when it comes to our understanding of mental illness.

I have to confess that at first, I was just as guilty of this ignorance. I was raised in a happy family with happy parents. There was no mental illness. There were no addictive personalities. I was totally clueless and unprepared for the traumas that awaited me after I married into a family with an alcoholic history. My mother-in-law was also bi-polar and later psychotic and it never even occurred to me that any of my children might inherit a genetic predisposition. When the illness first showed itself in Nate, he was about 13 years old. It just looked like immaturity to me. I would get exasperated with him but that didn't work. I would try to reason with him but that didn't work. We eventually brought him to counsellors but that didn't work either. Nothing seemed to work. It is the most awful thing in the world to watch a child spiral down into an emotional oblivion and be unable to do anything about it. I hate powerlessness. I hate it more than anything else.

But all this was followed by friends and acquaintances wagging their heads and saying, "You must have done something wrong." I was amazed by the eagerness with which people arrived at this conclusion. And yet, I was there everyday for my kids. I greeted them when they got home from school, helped them with their homework, took them to my art shows, cheered them on at their sporting events. We built Lego spaceships and told grizzly bear stories and went on scavenger hunts. I sang them to sleep at night with my guitar. I did everything my parents did when they raised me but the results were very different and... demoralizing.

So, if there is a lesson in all of this, perhaps it could be summed up with one word: Grace. It's a word that is sprinkled throughout this book. When you see someone suffering with mental illness or you see parents trying their best to deal with a child who is suffering, please don't wag your heads. Please don't automatically assume some evil has been committed. Just offer grace. It won't fix the fundamental problem, but it will show the kind of compassion and solidarity that is so often missing in a society that just doesn't understand.

6

Still Standing

Shortly after Nathaniel died, a young man wrote to me to say that he had decided to end his life. He felt he had let his family down. His siblings were successful but he was failing in school and struggling with anxiety. He was also far from home in an unfamiliar culture and he just felt lost. He was in his 20s and I was in my 60s. He was Muslim and I was Christian. He was also 12,000 miles away from me. But despite these things, I felt close to him. He was so respectful and sensitive. He called me 'Mr. Will'. The more I listened to him, the more I suspected he was a square peg in a round hole. By that I mean, his parents expected him to get a business degree but his gifts were in another field.

We had some deep conversations about heartache and how to find joy in the middle of it. We kept meeting online and sharing our experiences. I eventually asked him if I could give him two assignments and told him they were simple ones. I just wanted some clarity about what his gifts were and so the first assignment was for him to take a short personality test at the Meyers/Briggs website. I told him it would be an affirming experience because after answering some questions, he would be given an idea of who he really was and how best to use his talents. I also told him that it doesn't matter if we fail at a million things. Our goal is to discover the one talent that brings us joy and to nurture it. I knew my friend excelled in music and he loved filmmaking and I suspected that he belonged in a creative profession.

I've often thought that our talents are like buried treasure. We don't come with an instruction manual that tells us what they are. We're forced to look for them. There's a reason for this. The journey of discovery is as important as the treasure itself. On that journey we learn all kinds of things about ourselves. We learn about our weaknesses so we can understand the value of humility and grace. And in time, an inventory of talent appears that will define us and bring us joy. My new friend was eager to take the test.

His second assignment was to find someone at the very bottom of his society - someone who was treated as worthless by everyone else... and I asked him to do something loving for him. I asked him to maybe bring a meal to a homeless person and to treat the man with dignity. I asked my friend to absorb the whole moment as if the event had eternal significance and to look fully into the person's face as if he was looking into the face of God himself.

There was a pause and then my friend said, "That is the most beautiful thing I have ever heard. I will do it, Mr. Will. It is my promise to you. I will do it."

Before I tell you what happened next, I want to share something I experienced a few years after my first son died. I was exhibiting at an art show in Pennsylvania when a woman approached me. We shared a few pleasantries and then she told me that she was a funeral director and our conversation meandered towards the topic of grief. I told her that before I lost a child, no one expected great things from me but a few years after the loss, people seemed to respect everything I said. I told her I was puzzled by that.

The woman replied, "Will, people don't respect you because you lost a child. They respect you because you're still standing."

I felt instantly embarrassed because I had actually been through ten years of hell and I knew I hadn't handled things very well at first. I don't think anyone would have complimented me on how well I was "standing" back then.

I've been sitting in a home all by myself for 16 years now. I spent 25 years loving a wife and raising a family. It included a hectic, but fulfilling routine of taxiing my kids everywhere, homework help, romantic weekends with my wife, sporting events, music lessons, clothes shopping, birthday parties - the whole thing. There was barely time to stop and think. Then everything came to an end. An unfaithful wife, dead kids, pain and heartache and destruction everywhere I looked. In times of despair, it's so hard to believe that we will ever find joy again. I didn't handle it well. When we suffer a traumatic loss, it's like a bomb exploding in our neighborhood. We can't think clearly and no one can really say anything to us because all we can hear is the ringing in our ears.

When I look back at how I handled my pain, I realize that I felt more insecure than when I was a teenager. It felt like I was walking on a world made of jello because nothing seemed steady. It's hard to find your balance when everything is wobbly. Eventually I found my bearings and began to sense that I was being led to a place of beauty that is only available to broken souls.

One day I wrote a letter to myself. It contained three pieces of advice that I needed to follow if I was going to prevail...

1. *You need to know who you are.* You are not who cruel people say you are. Stop trying to be loved by them because they are incapable of love. Focus on your gifts. Those are the things that define you. Those are the reasons you breathe. You are Sensitive. Kind. Committed. Analytical. Devoted. Focus on who you are and forget the others. You are cherished by the ones who matter.

2. *Pain isn't meaningless.* It deepens us. It can have a beautiful, redemptive, purpose in our lives if we let it. It compels us to ask the most significant questions we could ever ask. It increases our capacity to love. Without pain, we can't learn compassion. Suffering can lead us to a place of emotional and spiritual maturity. It tells us, "It's ok to be human. It's ok to fail. It's ok to hurt. It's ok to be weak." Take it all in. Let the journey work its wonders in you. Ask the big questions. Be willing to laugh at yourself when you do dumb things. Just know that this pain will bring depth, maturity, compassion, and those things will eventually lead to joy. When pain and hope make love, indecipherable things become known.

3. *Give yourself to another suffering person and love them unconditionally.* For me, that meant adopting Jenny. This is where healing happens. There is a verse in Isaiah 58 that says, *"If you pour yourself out for the hungry and satisfy the desires of the afflicted, then shall your light rise in the darkness and your gloom be as the noonday sun.'"*[5]

These three discoveries lead us out of 'the dark night of the soul.' Discover who you are. Discover the purpose of pain. Discover the joy of loving another wounded person.

When my friend on the other side of the world was contemplating suicide, it was because he felt powerless. That sense of powerlessness came from not knowing yet who he truly was or that there was a treasure hidden inside him. Once he realized that he was not defined by what others expected of him but rather by who he was created to be, there was hope. After I gave him his two assignments, he later told me that he went into town and sat beside a homeless man. He took an interest in another wounded soul and began caring for someone who had been discarded. He later told me the experience had transformed him. Six months later, my friend shared one of my posts on social media and added, "These words saved my life."

We all hate trauma. We hate death. We hate losing loved ones. We hate betrayal and slander. But... the very things we hate, are the things that lead us to a place of depth, purpose and maturity and in the end, we are given the desires of our hearts. Perhaps this is why Washington Irving once wrote,

---
5   Isaiah 58:10

"There is sacredness in tears. They are not the mark of weakness, but of power. They speak more eloquently than ten thousand tongues. They are the messengers of overwhelming grief, of deep contrition and of unspeakable love."

7

The Sacrament of Grief

Imagine you are standing on a hillside near the ocean and beside you is a giant barrel of water. You push the barrel over and immediately the water gushes out, crashes into the sand and carves a deep channel into the hillside as it makes its way down to the ocean. Afterwards, whenever it rains, water will naturally flow into that channel and with each new storm, a deeper and deeper pathway will be cut.

When trauma is experienced, a similar process occurs in the human brain. A devastating event in our lives can create a neurological pathway of grief and anxiety and with each new trauma, the pathway becomes more and more determinative until we find ourselves gravitating towards fear, anguish and little else. Suddenly we are caught in a dilemma. On the one hand, pain must be processed because burying it or denying it is unhealthy. But on the other hand, if our thoughts are forever being driven into that channel, the mind will eventually be programmed to experience a hopeless cycle of despair. Our perspective on life will become distorted and our ability to find meaning in our suffering or to feel any joy at all will be lost.

There is a growing body of evidence suggesting that we can also carry the traumatic memories of our ancestors within our DNA. My adopted daughter's grandmother was physically and emotionally abused by her husband. That trauma produced an anxiety disorder in the grandmother which was then passed down to the next two generations. Trauma doesn't just alter one person's brain chemistry. It can impact the genetic propensities of several future generations. When we offer grace to a wounded soul and aid them in their journey of healing, we may be helping more than just our friend. We may be offering kindness to generations still to come.

All this points to a compelling truth: the brain is a miraculous organ but it's also incredibly vulnerable. For healing to happen, alternate pathways in the brain must be formed so that hopeful propensities can be reestablished. It's hard to do this at first, and might require only baby steps but the good news is that the more we endeavor to look for meaning and purpose, the easier that endeavor becomes.

When I lost a child, the first year of grieving was the hardest because I would experience something and immediately think, "I should tell Justin about this." My brain hadn't yet adjusted to the awful reality of his death. But then the truth would hit me: I can't tell my son anything. I can't have a conversation with him for the rest of my life. That shock would be felt over and over again during the first year. Eventually I stopped being surprised by his death and slowly began accepting what once seemed impossible to accept.

On some days I was little more than a sobbing mess. But

usually by the following day, after all the grief was released, I was able to be functional and productive again. It's important that we allow ourselves those cathartic moments. It's important that we give ourselves that grace.

If you are someone who is now experiencing that first year of grieving, I would like to tell you that it's not always going to be this way. Every year will not be like the first year. You will become someone new.

By the end of the first year, I began to experience resilience. I began to surprise myself. There is something about the human spirit that longs to make sense of our losses. I started to look for meaning in all the sadness. As new pathways were being formed in my brain, a sanctuary was created in my soul. I'm told that a sacrament is a 'visible manifestation of an invisible reality'. I think I was coming to realize that pain has the power to produce depth and depth has the power to produce a previously unimaginable joy. I knew that I needed to reinforce this process so it became my focus.

Nikita Gill has written a tender description of grief's stages…

> "Grief's firstborn child is Anger. She who storms from room to room, windows rattling in her wake, destruction her middle name, and she does not apologize for it. Hurricane in your chest, storm in your soul, she won't release you till you shatter.
>
> Grief's second child is Sadness. She who crawls inside your bones and stretches her ivy hands till every part of you is constricted inside this web of torment.

Tragedy in your bones, decay in your sinews, she will stay until you learn how to use the knife which cuts your way out.

Grief's youngest child is Healing. She who mends souls with lacquered gold, each crack glimmering in the sunlight. You will ask her why. Balm for your wounds, gentle rain for your spirit, she will tell you that what you have grieved was never meant to be forgotten."[6]

I believe grief prepares us for something beautiful and that breaking is how we become whole. If it's true, even our deepest wounds can have meaning. All the traumas, all the pain, all the betrayals, all the disappointments can become like fertile fields where wisdom is grown. Those fields aren't just preparing us to be healed. They are preparing us to be healers as well and once that truth fills us, hopelessness and cynicism seem to dissipate like a mist. This is when we know that we have been transformed. The absence of our loved ones will still be felt but now that absence is accompanied by a renewed sense of purpose. We are ready to wrap our arms around the next grieving soul, offer her grace, and find comfort in all the tenderness those moments will hold.

---

[6] Nikita Gill www.Facebook.com/nikitagillwrites

8

Every Square Inch

My dad was an artist who made his living near New York City. He painted the portraits of wealthy people and often commented on the subtleties of fine art. One day he told me that if I looked closely at the paintings of the great masters, I would see all the colors of the spectrum in every square inch. This is what gives a portrait its richness and its depth. It's also the thing that distinguishes the work of a genius from that of an amateur.

What looks simple from afar, is often quite complicated. A self portrait of Rembrandt shows the ruddy face of an aging man. From a distance we see only flesh tones. But when we step closer to the canvas, another world opens up to us. There are greens, purples, yellows, blues and grays applied to the face with such mastery and we marvel at the complexity of it all.

When I was young, my dad also taught me that our actions have consequences. There was something comforting and predictable about that idea. I saw my dad being faithful to my mom and I saw her returning the love. It was the natural consequence of a tender relationship. I didn't always agree with my dad on matters of faith or politics but he was an honorable man and he loved me. He provided for his family and took an interest in our lives. When he died, his children cried and my mom knew she had lost her soulmate. It was all so predictable.

But my greatest disappointment in life was realizing that very little is predictable. Not every devoted spouse is rewarded with faithfulness. Not every child cries at the death of a committed parent. Sometimes children rebel against even the most basic requests for decency. Other times, a loving son or daughter will die in our arms. Ours is a life where sweet, caring friends succumb to cancer and intolerable people live to a ripe old age. It leaves us wondering, "How can any of this make sense? Why do good people suffer? Why do the wicked prosper? Where is the logic and predictability of life? ...and why are all those colors on Rembrandt's face?"

After a while, I began to wonder whether our lives are like a portrait being painted by a renaissance artist. If our eyes are too close to the canvas, we might be confused by its complexity and wonder, "What crazy person would put every color of the spectrum in every square inch?" Our souls will focus on disappointing things and we will ask a lot of haunting questions that seem to have no answer. Most importantly, we won't be able to make sense of the entire work of art because we are too close to the pain.

It can take years before we're able to comprehend the meaning of life's traumas. It isn't until we view things from a distance that we begin to make sense of our own portraits.

Those confusing colors are like the heartbreaking events of our lives - the very things that deepen us and stimulate the formation of a beautiful soul. They are what make our personal renaissance (rebirth) possible. A Native American named Vine Deloria Jr. once said, *"Religion is for people who are afraid of hell, spirituality is for people who have already been there."*

If we never experience the rude disappointments of life, it is nearly impossible for us to have the richness and depth that a masterful artist seeks to create. We will offer only trite and shallow 'answers' to a world that yearns for something more. Someone once said that fundamentalism is to faith what paint-by-numbers is to the Renaissance. It presents a portrait of the divine that does the opposite of what it's supposed to do. It oversimplifies the complex. Augustine said it another way, *"If you can comprehend it, it is not God."*

Sometimes I think I have two lives. During the day, I am happy. I spend my time creating things and it distracts me from my past. But at night, I lay in bed and a broken record begins playing in my head. It is a soundtrack of betrayal and loss and 30 years building a family that no longer exists. Sometimes it seems like I have wasted too many years. There are things about our lives that are difficult to understand - like the odd colors on Rembrandt's face or the pigments of a divine genius.

If it were possible to have our souls painted by a renaissance artist, strange colors in strange places would appear on the canvas - each one emblematic of the events that broke us and deepened us. The richness and depth of our portraits would be reflective of a faith that has matured. It is not a paint-by-number faith. It doesn't expect easy answers. It's not intellectually lazy. It longs to uncover deeper and deeper layers of truth. It never attempts to domesticate God. It is wonder-struck by the mysteries that surround us. All these things bear witness to the genius of a divine painter who is still at work in us.

As I'm writing these things, Jenny is messaging me. I would not have even met her if the tragedies of my life had never occurred. She tattooed my initials to her arm and she's saying, "I love you infinity times infinity." Maybe nothing is wasted. Maybe heartaches are what make redemption possible. Maybe life, with all its traumas can be beautiful anyway - like a rich, renaissance painting with every color of the spectrum in every square inch.

9

Live Everything

A friend of mine recently lost her baby. I've been wondering what to say because words seem so inadequate but today I remembered a tender experience. A few months after I lost Justin, something happened to me that filled me with wonder and brought me some solace. I'll share the experience now because sooner or later we all find ourselves grieving over a terrible loss and asking questions that have no answers. This is for my friend, Mónica and anyone else who has lost a child. I hope these thoughts will feel like a hug from a kindred spirit...

Justin used to say two words quite often. The words were "Live everything." His friends didn't know where the quote had come from and neither did I, but it meant something important to him.

A few months later, I found a small leather-bound book in a box of his belongings. It was a journal he had used to write down quotes that meant a lot to him. One of the quotes was from Rainer Maria Rilke (Letters to a Young Poet)...

"You are so young, so before all beginning, I want to beg you, as much as I can, to be patient toward all that is unsolved in your heart and to try to love the questions themselves like locked rooms and like books that are written in a very foreign tongue. Do not now seek the answers, which cannot be given you because you would not be able to live them. And the point is, to live everything. Live the questions now. Perhaps you will then gradually without noticing it, live along some distant day into the answer."[7]

I remember when Justin was an infant, I would take him in my arms and tell the world, "This is my son!" I was so proud. Twenty-five years later, after receiving his cremated remains, I sat down on my bedroom floor and took the bag of ashes from the box. As I held those eight pounds of silence in my arms and rocked him back and forth, I couldn't help but think that there is such a deep yearning in the human spirit to make sense of it all....

In a previous book, I wrote these words:

"Maybe we just want to bring order to chaos. Maybe we think that if we understand the indecipherable, we can make our lives secure. But sometimes our journey brings us to a place where we love the questions even more than their elusive answers because the questions teach us humility and brokenness, which in turn, leads us to a place we could otherwise never find."[8]

---
[7] Rainer Maria Rilke, trans. John L.L. Mood, *Rilke on Love and Other Difficulties* (New York: W.W. Norton, 1975) 25.
[8] K.William Kautz, Winter's Grace (Denver: Outskirts Press, 2012) 7.

When I read that Rilke quote, it made me realize something important: the most beautiful and redemptive lessons in life are delivered to us through pain. When we are comfortable and content, we don't bother to go deep. But the good stuff is hidden in the deep stuff and we can't get it without some measure of suffering. I've also noticed that all of my favorite people have been wounded. They have all been made tender and alluring because their souls experienced trauma.

Before Monica lost her son, she wrote something on her Facebook page: "Those who know me know that I drown in shallow waters." Deep waters may be scary, but to her, they will never be as scary as a shallow, meaningless life. Most people don't want to be "in over their heads" but her soul requires it. That's a gift. It might sometimes seem like a curse precisely because depth almost always comes from pain but... I suspect that she is lovable precisely because when she experiences pain, she turns it into something of value for those around her.

I've also seen from her videos an ability to encourage others. She has a confident spirit. It's not a presumptuous confidence. It is probably borne from grief. I think in time, everyone who learns to "live everything" and to love the unanswerable questions finds what they are looking for: there is meaning in suffering because the most heartbreaking experiences of our lives have a way of producing the most sensitive and transformational movements in our souls.

So as we swim in the depths of those unanswerable questions, we are becoming who we were meant to be. It hurts. But it's not meaningless. In fact, it's full of glory and grace. Augustine once noticed that those questions have a way of drawing us into the arms of Someone who calls us his 'beloved' and who created us for intimacy. So I'll end this chapter with some words that he once prayed which mean a lot to me:

> *"In my deepest wound I saw your glory and it dazzled me."*

10

Maligne Lake

My adopted daughter is a tender soul whose childhood was filled with uncertainty and fear. One day, after becoming her dad, I wrote a letter to her because I wanted to acknowledge those fears and at the same time encourage her to see all the beauty that her difficult past had produced in her. She has allowed me to share that letter here...

Dear Jenny,

I want to show you a photo of my favorite place in the world. It is a long, thin, sliver of a lake in northern Alberta - tucked away in the Canadian Rockies - a few hours north of the Columbia Ice Fields.

The last time I was there, I overheard a woman ask a question to her friend. She said, "How can anyone look at this and deny the existence of God?"

I believe in a Creator, but the skeptic in me knows that other people would ask a different question: "If beauty proves God, does ugliness disprove him? Does evil and inhumanity and suffering and death prove that a loving God couldn't possibly exist?"

But after realizing the futility of these questions, I found another one whose answer might satisfy us with a beautiful and compelling truth.

That question is... What misery had to happen before this place could mesmerize us? After all, its scenery wasn't always awe-inspiring. Its terrain was once flat. Its lake didn't exist. There were no elk and deer. There were no creatures at all.

Geologists tell us that the Pacific plate of the earth's crust began pushing under the North American plate with such violence and power that millions of tons of rock were shoved thousands of feet into the air. It took trauma and brute force to form these mountains. And the violence didn't end there. For thousands of years this place was a frozen, desolate, uninhabitable wasteland. No one would have wanted to visit it. The ice age covered the soil with glaciers that were thousands of feet thick. The earth beneath was scarred and scraped mercilessly by the weight of frozen rivers. Huge boulders were shoved thousands of miles south. Deep ravines were carved between mountain ridges. Rocks were pulverized into powder under the weight of the ice. The powder is so fine that it is now called "glacial flour".

Do you see the color of the water? The first time I saw it, I couldn't believe my eyes. It is a glorious, translucent, aquamarine - caused by the sun reflecting off of the glacial flour as it sits suspended in the water.

Even the colors would not be possible without trauma and violence.

This place speaks to me like no other. Its lessons aren't merely geological. They are spiritual. What if real beauty isn't possible without suffering? What if maturity - the ability to feel compassion for broken, vulnerable people - could never be ours unless we first experience the pain of an inconceivable loss? What if God is far more interested in making us beautiful than in making us comfortable? What if we could never dispense grace to another human being until we first experienced the wrath and judgment of merciless people? What if all the disordered miseries of this world were actually being transformed into something meaningful by some redeeming power - like a consuming fire that burns away our dross - leaving only gold? What if all pain has purpose - if only we let it?

It has been eight years since you became my daughter. In that short time, I have come to see that your beautiful soul has everything to do with the heartaches of your childhood. Your transparency and humility, your teachable spirit and your gratitude, your devotion to me even when you couldn't understand a few of my decisions - they all speak of your character. You have a beauty and a tenderness that reminds me of an alpine lake. It is deep and enduring because it has been formed by terrible loss and humiliating pain.

Jenny Isabella, Maligne Lake used to be my favorite place in the world but now that place is you. Thank you for picking me for your dad. My greatest honor was forged in the crucible of my greatest loss. It seems to be the nature of all things.

    Love, Dad

11

Liquid Love and Loneliness

A few years ago I read about a teenager in Florida who was born with a rare disorder. She was fully functional in every way. She was intelligent. She was agile. She was social. But she couldn't feel physical pain. We might think, "I want what she has." But it isn't that simple. Someone could burn her with a cigarette lighter and she wouldn't even feel it.

Her mom also noticed that the girl was incapable of empathy. If we never experience pain, we have no reference point to go to when another person is hurting. Our souls don't understand. We simply cannot become mature, loving adults without the experience of suffering. And without maturity, we are left feeling alienated from everything that is meaningful. In other words, painlessness produces the misery of a shallow life and painfulness enables the joy of loving deeply.

...and there's the paradox. It's an awe-filled mystery that calls to us from the deepest trenches of our souls. It seems odd that the answer to humanity's most agonizing question might be hidden in the inquiry itself: *"Why God? Why God? Why God? WHY?"* Depth, maturity and compassion often flow from that one haunting question. Yet how many times have we heard someone say, "I don't want anything to do with a God who allows suffering"? That's like a kid saying, "I don't want anything to do with a parent who desires maturity in me."

One of my favorite authors is Henri Nouwen. Nouwen was a master at writing little books that were packed full of meaning. He died a few years ago and after his death, I discovered that he had struggled in secret with a painful situation through much of his life. Once I learned that, the depth of his writings made perfect sense. There is something about suffering that beckons a person towards a sacred place where we are able to identify with lost and broken souls. In his book, "The Wounded Healer," Nouwen says

> *"Compassion asks us to go where it hurts, to enter into the places of pain, to share in brokenness, fear, confusion, and anguish. Compassion challenges us to cry out with those in misery, to mourn with those who are lonely, to weep with those in tears. Compassion requires us to be weak with the weak, vulnerable with the vulnerable, and powerless with the powerless. Compassion means full immersion in the condition of being human."*[9]

---

9   Henri Nouwen, The Wounded Healer (New York: Image/Doubleday, 1972)

Last week, I received a sweet comment from a friend named Juliana Momodu. She described something I wrote by saying, "It is a narrative written with a pen whose ink is liquid love." That's the way I feel about Henri Nouwen's words.

A person who has felt intense pain has been trained to love more deeply. She has been sensitized to the needs of others. It is as if her spiritual nerve endings have been so uncovered and exposed that she is now able to identify and empathize with the most vulnerable among us. What position in this world could be more noble than that?

During the past few weeks, I have received thousands of comments and hundreds of private messages from people all over the world. Some are suffering from mental illness. Others are in anguish over their children's suffering. Every one of these people knows what it means to scream in the dark. They have felt the pain of loneliness and the scorn of those who distort their characters and demean their humanity. The loneliest kind of loneliness isn't the kind that we feel when we're alone. It is the kind that is felt when we are in the company of those who devalue us. Very often this leads to self-hatred and yet, as Henri Nouwen so beautifully writes, *"Self-rejection is the greatest enemy of the spiritual life because it contradicts the sacred voice that calls us the Beloved."*

I am convinced that the voices that truly matter are the ones that cry in the wilderness. Your grief doesn't make you worthless. It makes you priceless. You have something to offer because you've suffered. There are bone-dry deserts ready to be watered and fields of wheat ready to be harvested with the wisdom you've acquired. Why? Because people are hungering for more than deceitful political promises or the liturgies of stale religion. Once we have suffered, we understand that broken cisterns and scum-filled buckets can never quench our thirst. Only a fountain of living water can do that.

And that's the point, isn't it? It is the intersection of pain and purpose where the stuff of eternity resides.

PART TWO – GRACELAND

12

Love Beneath the Veil

There are some spiritual traditions that tell us a veil exists between the perfect and the imperfect and that beneath that veil, we can only catch momentary glimpses of life on the other side. Beneath the veil, we see imperfectly and reason imperfectly and love imperfectly. To live beneath the veil is to ache with a hunger that can only be partially satisfied. Here, we experience loss and uncertainty and try to make sense of it all and in our own feeble ways, we discover our world to be like a grand incubator - preparing us for something yet unseen. And so we stumble from trauma to trauma with moments of ecstasy sandwiched in between and gradually, over time, we reluctantly acknowledge that all of it has meaning. It has deepened our character and increased our yearning for those things that truly matter.

But how do we love *ourselves* beneath the veil? How do we accept ourselves after a failure or when we feel inadequate, unloved or even unworthy? How do we care for our own souls when we are filled with doubt or shame?

The other day I poked an old CD into my car stereo and began listening to Paul Simon's Graceland...

> *"Losing love is like a window in your heart,*
> *Everybody sees you're blown apart*
> *Everybody feels the wind blow.*
> *I'm going to Graceland, Graceland, Graceland.*
> *I have reason to believe we all will be received in Graceland."*

Those words reminded me of a time when I was a mess. I was blinded by grief after my family had been destroyed and I made some really poor choices. More than anything else, I was defined by a startling sense of insecurity.

It was hard acknowledging my limitations. It was hard dealing with people who are incapable of remorse. It was hard trying to love someone whose conscience was dead. We can leave such people behind but the heartache remains long after they're gone from our lives. Sometimes we find ourselves in impossible positions where we're damned if we do and damned if we don't. It was too much for me and I crumbled under the weight of it.

Back then, I used to have recurring nightmares where I was filled with shame but I couldn't understand why. I would dream that I was sitting in church completely naked when everyone else was dressed. I'd wake up from those dreams with my heart pounding so hard I could actually hear it with my ears. This was back in the days when I presumed church to be a place of refuge even though it wasn't. The minister didn't know how to love people who were hurting. He was a good public speaker but he could never be a pastor because he had no empathy. He would wag his head and imagine the worst about people. At the same time, he was preaching about grace but he couldn't live it. I don't think any of us can live it until we've been brought to our knees.

During this time, a member of my church was hit by a car. After emerging from a coma, he wasn't able to function the way he used to. He was a sweet guy but he would do awkward things like handing out roses to strangers in the pews and sometimes people would feel uncomfortable. He didn't do anything immoral but it was difficult to know how to respond to him. The minister preferred to believe that the man was failing spiritually when the real issue was neurological damage caused by the accident. The situation required compassion but one Sunday, it was announced that the man was not permitted to attend church until he corrected his behavior. That was the moment I realized I needed to leave. I left after the announcement was made and never looked back. I guess I was leaving for Graceland.

But where do we find Graceland and what does it look like? I used to spend hours alone asking myself those questions. One day I thought of an illustration that could provide an answer and help me to never forget...

I told myself to think of two friends who seemed to have it all together. They were happy, successful, loving and mature. Then I asked myself to think of two friends who were difficult to be with. They were negative, emotionally unstable, unproductive and self-absorbed. Then I imagined a large vat of boiling water and I thought, "What would happen if all four of those friends were thrown into that vat by some uncontrollable twist of fate? What would I see? Would the two mature friends have peaceful looks on their faces? Would the two immature friends be screaming bloody murder and begging for mercy? ...or would all FOUR of those people be in so much pain that their responses would be indistinguishable? Wouldn't they all look the same in their anguish?

Grace is something that happens when we finally realize how vulnerable we all are and that no one is invincible. If any one of us is subjected to enough grief, we will crumble. And when we do, we will make mistakes that can't be undone. We will scream and do dumb things and fail to think clearly. After that, the shame comes - followed by a longing to be loved despite it all.

Carl Jung once wrote, *"But what if I should discover that the least among them all, the poorest of all beggars, the most impudent of all offenders, yea the very fiend himself - that these are within me, and that I myself stand in need of my own kindness, that I myself am the enemy who must be loved - what then? Then, as a rule, the whole truth of Christianity is reversed: there is no more talk of love and long-suffering; we say to the brother within us, "Raca," and condemn and rage against ourselves. We hide him from the world; we deny ever having met this least among the lowly in ourselves, and had it been God himself who drew near to us in this despicable form, we should have denied him a thousand times before a single cock had crowed."*[10]

Every time we buckle ourselves into an airplane the flight attendant reminds us that in case of an emergency, we should secure our own air supply before we help another. We can't

---
10 Carl Jung, *Memories, Dreams, Reflections* (New York: Vintage Books, 1989)

help anyone if we can't even breathe. Grace is like an air supply that's offered to us by the Lover of our souls. He says, "Here, take this. Breathe it all in. You are loved. You are cherished. It's ok to hurt. It's ok to make mistakes. I have prepared something beautiful for you. I am bringing you on this journey because you are priceless to me."

I don't think we ever really question the sacred. We question the perversion of sacred things. We question stale religion when it becomes a cheap substitute for a sacrificial life. We question the motivation of those who replace love with dogma. We question rituals that dull the conscience - as if a few dollars thrown into an offering plate can anesthetize the soul against the emptiness of a self-centered life. But the sacred still remains and the yearning for meaning will always fill us until the other side of the veil calls us home.

Sometimes I lie in bed at night and imagine God quoting Shakespeare to me:

> "Doubt thou the stars are fire;
> Doubt that the sun doth move;
> Doubt truth to be a liar;
> But never doubt I love."[11]

This is why I'm going to Graceland, Graceland, Graceland. You can come with me if you'd like. I have reason to believe we all will be received in Graceland.

---

11   William Shakespeare, Hamlet

13

Someone I Love

Once we have forgiven ourselves and accepted our vulnerabilities, we become uniquely qualified to share that grace with others. Last week, someone I love almost ended her life. She panicked in a moment of hopelessness and couldn't think about the consequences. She survived the experience and is healing now but she's also filled with shame. I know she'll overcome this but I want to offer a few thoughts about how to love a person when their pain distorts everything and they begin to lose sight of what's real.

I remember when I was a young father, I would hold a baby in my arms and be amazed at how helpless she was. The only thing she could do was burp up curdled milk on my shoulders and make messes in her diaper but if anything, her helplessness only made me love her more. My love was defined by the joy of being able to protect and cherish and believe in the potential of someone who was incapable of doing anything for herself.

Whenever I am tempted to beat myself up over any

mistake, I try to remember those days as a young father. I didn't expect perfection from my kids and I don't think God expects it from us either. I've made mistakes that only a fool would make. There were times when I felt insecure about my place in this world and about all those people who could have loved me but didn't. At times I was so blinded by the pain that I couldn't think straight. I should have known better than to accept the terms that were offered by unhealthy people but I accepted them anyway. I wish I had been wise. I wish I could have spared myself all the shame. But the truth is, wisdom only comes from failure.

When we beat ourselves up, we miss the point of grace. Grace is the love that's offered to us even when we're weak. It is the love that says, "Yes, you faltered but you're still precious to me." Grace is the thing that forms the basis of all personal growth. We are worthy of love not because we're perfect but because we have been created for deep, loving relationships that are only made possible by the wisdom that comes to us through laments and regrets.

I once put one of my sons on a changing table and he peed in my face. All I could do was laugh and love the little rascal even more. Whenever I held him in my arms, I never expected him to give me clean diapers. I knew his first accomplishments wouldn't smell like roses. I'm convinced that this is the way God views us when we are overcome with pain or are embarrassed by our own inadequacies. He knows we aren't perfect. He knows our grief can blind us. It's not the failures that matter. It's the growth that follows.

It's also important to remember that our entire lives aren't spent in dark valleys or dangling above some frightening abyss. We are given periods of rest after a time of trial so that we can consider all the way we've come and the lessons we've learned. There is comfort in that truth. Our traumas don't last forever. There are spiritual vacations filled with joy that await us after a time of intense sorrow. These are times to meditate on what is true and to consider what gold remains after the dross is burned away.

Years ago, a teacher called me a gifted writer but I didn't think I had anything to say. I wanted to use my talent but I was young and immature and life hadn't humbled me yet. It was my failures that gave me something to say. It was the time spent in darkness that caused me to value the complexities of life and all the answers I didn't have. We learn to go deep after we realize that the luxury and comfort of a self-satisfied life stunts our growth. That's when the joy appears because all the miseries of life and all of our embarrassing mistakes brought us to this place of grace. Suddenly we realize that our shortcomings are actually things of immeasurable worth because they humble us and remove the blinders from our eyes. Forgiveness comes easy after that because we finally realize that what defines us isn't our failures but how we responded to them.

14

Facing the Deep

I discovered a British artist recently named Stephanie Rew whose portraits speak to me about the frailty and power that defines each of us. Often, her paintings display pensive, inquisitive faces that appear to ask "Who am I?" In one sketch, a woman seems afraid to face her fears and yet the gilding around her shoulders suggests she is clothed in an unknown splendor. In many ways, it is a portrait of the human soul. We can be full of pain and apprehension and at the same time, oblivious to our own pricelessness.

I have an old friend who was demeaned by her mother and father throughout her childhood. As an adult, she continued to receive the constant negative comments of her two unhappy parents. I knew about the pain she carried. I knew she had never been affirmed. I also knew that she wasn't able to express sorrow when she hurt someone else. I think in my friend's mind, saying the words, "I'm sorry" was the same as saying, "I'm worthless." I suspected that her pain and her inability to examine herself honestly were connected.

One evening I was invited to dinner while her father was visiting. My friend was an excellent cook. Every meal she created was prepared with love. So that night, after the meal was over, I tried to coax a compliment from her father. I said, "Ruben, what did you think of the dinner your daughter made?" I just wanted my friend to hear one kind word from her father. She was in the next room and could hear her dad's reply. He said, "It made me gag."

Over the years, I've come to realize that before we can summon the strength to examine our behaviors and to search for healing, we first need to plumb the depths of our own pricelessness. We need to ask, "Who am I?" and find some affirming way to answer that question. If we doubt our own value, it will be too painful to examine our weaknesses or those areas of our lives that require attention.

So where does our worth come from? I believe we have all been 'wondrously and fearfully made' in the image of a loving God but I also understand that there are some who have no faith and others who seem inconsolable. For those beautiful souls, there is a way to begin the healing process. A tender connection with a grace-filled person can lead us towards an understanding of our own immeasurable worth and gradually, as we discard our pretenses and embrace humility, we can finally acknowledge the consequences of our wounds. It requires courage but eventually we will realize that it doesn't matter how much we might have blundered. What matters is that we are capable of a deep, spiritual intimacy with someone if we would only allow it.

It is, after all, our endearing capacity for intimacy that makes us priceless.

My old friend couldn't muster that courage. I think she had been so hurt by years of humiliation that she just wasn't willing to do battle with the demons that haunted her. She preferred to be in denial of the wounds within. She would tell me that she wasn't damaged by her past and that she was stronger because of it. But the pain she inflicted on people who loved her suggested otherwise. She needed healing but the process was too frightening for her.

After the English army was rescued from Dunkirk, Winston Churchill famously said, *"Wars are not won by evacuations."* An army can be saved by escaping defeat but battles must still be fought before any victories are achievable.

I'm convinced that healing only happens when we are able to do two things: embrace the wonder of our pricelessness and face the depth and consequences of our pain. "We repeat what we don't repair." Many people believe that their value is rooted in their talents but our choices are more important than any talent. All the talent in the world isn't going to help us if we choose to run away from our own healing. This is one of those times when courage is synonymous with integrity because *"Wars are not won by evacuations"* and there are few things more tragic than going through life unhealed. In his book, The Seven Storey Mountain, Thomas Merton wrote, *"Souls are like athletes, that need opponents worthy of them, if they are to be tried and extended and pushed to the full use of their powers, and rewarded according to their capacity."*[12]

No opponent has the ability to change us more than our own pain. If we understand our worth, pain has the power to deepen us and transform our souls into something beautiful. I

---

12   Thomas Merton, *The Seven Storey Mountain* (New York: Harcourt Brace, 1948)

am offering these words now because if you are someone in need of healing, I want you to know that you are worthy of the joy that awaits you if you would allow a friend or a grace-filled counselor to show you your pricelessness and love you through the healing process.

15

Courage

Many years ago, I was traveling through Pennsylvania with a friend who had experienced several childhood traumas. She had built an impenetrable wall around herself - never allowing her pain to show and never acknowledging any weakness. I suppose it was her way of feeling safe even though the strategy only added to her sorrow.

It was wintertime when we made our trip and a snowstorm had blown across the state a few days earlier. The plows had created huge snow banks on either side of the highway which made us feel like we were driving through a tunnel with no exits. I was in the passenger seat and my friend was driving. As the car began warming up, she decided to slip her arms out of her winter coat with one hand on the steering wheel. I didn't think it was a good idea because we were zipping down the interstate at 70 mph. I remember saying, "I wouldn't do that..." - just as my friend lost control of her car.

The little Honda Civic began careening toward the snow bank on the left side of the highway so my friend yanked the steering wheel too sharply to the right without braking. Predictably, the car raced towards the snow bank on the opposite side of the road. This craziness repeated itself over and over. The car zoomed to the left, then zoomed to the right, then zoomed to the left again and the other vehicles on the highway decided to give my companion all the room she needed. It's a scary thing to be sitting in an out-of-control car - especially when the driver has forgotten about the brakes. Finally, my friend let go of the steering wheel, threw her hands in the air and said, "It's not working! It's not working!"

The car careened one last time across the highway and slammed into the right snow bank, spun around until it was facing oncoming traffic, flipped onto its side and then slowly fell back on its wheels. There was a brief moment of silence as we realized we were both going to live and then I asked, "Would you like me to drive now?" For the next five hours I drove a car that worked perfectly despite the dents on the roof, hood, sides and back. Basically, every body panel on that Civic had a snow bank pushed into it but the engine and brakes were working fine.

Sometimes we make mistakes and our lives spin out of control. By the time we think to put on the brakes, it's often too late. But after it's over and the damage is done, we have an opportunity to reflect on what happened. An emotionally intelligent person will do that. A deeply wounded person often won't.

I felt sorry for my friend. She had been through hell as a child and as a result, had a terribly fragile sense of self. It always seemed impossible for her to face her pain, her inadequacies or her failures. When she screamed, "It's not working!

It's not working!" she was blaming the car for her own inexperience and this was the way she conducted all of her affairs. It's been many years since I've seen her. The last time we spoke, she was deflecting attention away from her mistakes and hurting anyone who asked her to be real.

Sometimes the most obvious truths are the most difficult to grasp - not because they are complicated, but because they are painful. Carl Jung once wrote, *"That which I most need to find will be found where I least want to look."*

I have great respect for people who have made a mistake and afterwards, demonstrated the kind of courage and humility that asks, "Why did I do this? What do I need to learn? Asking such questions is like a leap of faith. The more wounded we are, the greater the leap and the greater the need for courage.

But what if someone is in so much pain or is so frightened by difficult truths that self-examination (and healing) seem impossible? Could love make courage possible? After all, inadequacies and weaknesses aren't the only things that define a wounded person. Being lovable doesn't require perfection because there's that thing called 'grace.'

Grace is offered to us because we are more than a jumble of imperfections. There is something precious and priceless about us despite our flaws. Some people have a difficult time believing this but I'm convinced that if any of us is put under enough pressure, we will break. No one is invincible. Every one of us fails and everyone of us needs grace.

Forgiving ourselves, loving ourselves, understanding ourselves - these are things that happen when we begin to plumb the depths of God's grace. It takes courage to examine our weaknesses but if our examination is accompanied by an understanding of the deep love that God has for us, it becomes a liberating exercise because it leads us to the realization that grace isn't passive. We are adored by One who pursues us like a lover and offers us redemption.

One of my friends recently posted the following message on her social media account:

> "Shame says, 'Because I am flawed, I am unacceptable.' Grace says, 'Although I am flawed, I am cherished.'"

16

Wearing Masks

Every now and then, someone reminds me that nearly all of my readers on social media are women. When I'm asked why that is, I never know how to answer. It's kind of sweet but it's also embarrassing because for some reason, I'm not connecting with the other half of the human race.

I have a habit of baring my soul and I guess that conflicts with the usual image of a manly man. There's this thing called 'male toxicity'. It's a term used to describe how society tells boys and men that they have to be strong and they shouldn't show weakness and they should just 'suck it up.' The reason this is toxic is because it requires only a pretense of strength rather than the real thing. It also undermines loving, transparent relationships with women. And children. And other men.

But pretending to be strong isn't strength - it's weakness. Building an emotional fortress around ourselves doesn't make us look invincible - it makes us look like we're hiding. Real courage is about lowering the drawbridge and riding into the fray. If we aren't being real about our vulnerabilities, we're just engaging in a fraud that guarantees shallow, unfulfilling relationships with everyone.

Which brings me to a little story… Last December, I was given a commission to reproduce an antique locomotive weathervane. I've admired early American folk art for decades and I've made a living recreating it. The weathervane would be 5 feet long and very detailed. The original sold for $1.2 million at an auction in the 1990s. I was excited about the project and put my whole heart into it. I was going to earn $7500 and that money would get me through my usual winter slow season. When I finished it, I was really proud of myself. I had it professionally photographed and posted the photos on Instagram. All my Instagram followers began saying, "Wow! Incredible! That's AMAZING! Museum quality!"

Then I showed it to my customer. He didn't want it. He said the wrong number of spokes were on the wheels. I suspect he was having second thoughts about spending so much money and was looking for an excuse to get out of our agreement. So… I lost that sale and was pretty demoralized because all my work was in vain. In forty years I've never had someone cancel an order. That day, I was so bummed, I didn't want to talk to anyone. The next day, I was fantasizing with a friend about toilet papering the dude's house. By the third day, I messaged another friend and joked, "I have forgiven that scoundrel and no longer harbor any ill will towards his malevolent, God-forsaken, demon-infested soul." A week later, I had calmed down a little bit. Finally, after some time had passed, I began telling myself, "You're not homeless. All your needs are met. You're in good health. Everything's going to be fine."

Whenever I post one of my essays on Facebook, people tell me how wise I am but for me, wisdom is just an occasional thing. Sometimes I feel forsaken. Sometimes I sulk. Sometimes I blurt out stupid stuff. It kind of depends on what I'm going through at the moment. I can be articulate if I take the time to think things through but I can also be so unimpressive that people wag their heads at me.

When covid first hit, a pastor stood in a pulpit and said, "Some of you are angry about wearing masks but you've been doing it for years."

'Wearing masks' is what people do when they pretend to be something they're not. It's a scary thing to take off our masks and show the world that we aren't always strong, wise and hopeful. We think, "people might not like me if I admit to being merely human." But pretending only breeds phoniness and leaves us feeling emptied of the very thing we wanted most in life: a loving relationship with an authentic human being.

I used to read The Velveteen Rabbit to my kids. There's a passage in that story that speaks to our souls:

> "You become. It takes a long time. That's why it doesn't happen often to people who break easily, or have sharp edges, or who have to be carefully kept. Generally, by the time you are Real, most of your hair has been loved off, and your eyes drop out and you get loose in your joints and very shabby. But these things don't matter at all, because once you are real you can't be ugly, except to people who don't understand."[13]

---

13   Margery Williams, *The Velveteen Rabbit* (New York: Doubleday, 1958)

Sometimes life hits us hard and there is no instant healing - no instant wisdom. Those who lack empathy will expect perfection from us but our real friends will offer us grace. They are the ones we can bare our souls to when we feel unmoored and cast adrift. They will be the ones who will help us paddle back to shore - even when the currents are strong. If we can find friends like that, we won't need fortresses and armor because we'll be living in a culture of affirmation. There's no need for phoniness where grace and courage are present.

17

The Splendor of our Inadequacies

This past week I had the pleasure of talking with three people from very different cultures. One was a young person from Pakistan. Another was a lawyer from Kenya. The third was a retired person from Canada. Although so much was different about them, they all shared one common emotion: the fear of being vulnerable. Of course, their stories are our stories. We are all terrified of being fully exposed. And there are clearly times when it's appropriate to keep our guard up but… I would like to talk about those times when our walls should come down.

Before I do, I want to tell you about an experience I had when I was a young father. A few years before this experience, I had set several lofty goals for myself and reached them and I was feeling accomplished and invincible. Then I set a modest goal and failed completely. I spent the next year pouting. I was angry at myself and angry at the people who prevented me from reaching my goal. I also got myself into a deep blue funk and I began asking myself, "Why are we lovable even when we fail?"

I couldn't answer the question to my liking and that bothered me. I believed that God loves us but the actual reason behind it was a mystery. I would often think about my own failures and I'd be hard on myself. If we don't know why we are lovable, it is difficult to forgive anyone – especially ourselves. It is also difficult to be vulnerable to another human being.

Then one night, my 3-year-old daughter asked me to tuck her in bed. Emily was an adorable little girl. Squeezing her was one of my favorite things to do. So we climbed into bed with our Richard Scary book and spent the next half hour giggling. When it was time to kiss her good night and turn out the light, Emily said, "Daddy, will you stay with me until I fall asleep?" So I laid down next to her. Our heads were facing each other on the same pillow and I began to drift off into thought. The same old question haunted me. "What makes us lovable even when we fail?"

I'm not sure how much time passed but Emily didn't fall asleep. Apparently, she had been staring at me the whole time. Back then, whenever she wanted to get my attention, she would sandwich my face between her hands and look deeply into my eyes and say, "Daddy, look at me." But on that night, she put my face between her hands and said, "Daddy, do this." Then she put her two index fingers up her nose.

I obeyed her and Emily began laughing hysterically. In her mind, there was nothing funnier than a dad with his fingers up his nose.

I looked at her. She didn't have a care in the world. She was so sweet and vulnerable and real and she wasn't concerned about how silly she looked. I began to think, "I love this girl! There isn't anything I wouldn't do for her. I would run into a burning building to save her. I would give my life..."

And then I remembered something about Emily. She didn't always perform as well as her dad would like. In fact, just the day before, she had taken a stone from our driveway and scratched a smiley face into the side of our brand new car. A week before that, she made a beautiful picture with a green permanent marker on the wall-to-wall carpet in her bedroom. Then she ran downstairs, grabbed my hand and proudly brought me to her masterpiece.

As I thought about these things, I realized that I didn't care about the car. And I didn't care about the carpet. What I REALLY cared about was that I could have this tender, intimate relationship with a flawed but priceless little girl who gave me crazy experiences that made no sense at all but... she's mine. She's the joy of my life despite the imperfections and I would still die for her. Even if she grew up to scorn me, I would still love her with my dying breath.

What I learned from all of this is that perfection isn't possible but intimacy is. And that's what we were created for. Not perfection. Just intimacy. There is no joy in striving for perfection because we will always fail in that endeavor. But joyful, transformative intimacy is available to those who are willing to take down their walls, put their fingers up their noses, and say, "This is who I am – in all my glory and all my shame. I am really good at some things, but I suck at other things. Will you love me anyway? If I bare my soul to you, will you bare your soul to me?"

We have spent so many years of our lives cultivating a pretense of strength but redemption isn't found in strength. It is found in weaknesses – the very thing we have dreaded and denied. True, being vulnerable is terrifying but without it, we could never have the love we all yearn for.

After I lost my first son, I did some writing about anguish and grace and at one point I asked, *"What does it mean to be part of an authentic community where we are able to be REAL rather than phony, DEEP rather than shallow, STIMULATING rather than boring, FULL rather than empty? What does it mean to take off our masks and shed the pretense of invincibility or flawlessness and confess our weaknesses to others in an atmosphere of grace? By baring our souls, we encourage other authentic, healthy people to do the same. We create a culture of humility and grace where it is safe to be broken and honest and human."*[14]

This is why our inadequacies are so full of splendor. They teach us the value of humility, forgiveness and grace. Without these things, we wouldn't even know where to begin our search for anything deep. The most desirable trait that any of us could ever have is a broken and contrite heart. It is what makes flawed people so beautiful. It is also why we are called, "Beloved" by the Lover of our souls.

---

14 K. William Kautz, *Winter's Grace* (Denver: Outskirts Press, 2012)

18

Dying to Live

I've always been mesmerized by paradoxes. There's something about the power of being vulnerable or the triumph that comes from surrender that captivates me. When I see such things, I feel like a kid unwrapping a present. There must be something awesome inside. Why else would it be hidden?

One of the greatest of all paradoxes is this one:

"Unless a seed falls to the ground and dies, it can bear no fruit..."[15]

In one short sentence the entire dynamic of growth is revealed.

Thirty years ago I found myself in a debate with a Constitutional Law professor. It was in a lecture hall filled with 150 students and I lost that debate. It was a humbling experience but I needed it because I was young and cocky.

---

15   John 12:24

Before that debate I thought I had a solid grasp of the topic. But I was wrong and as I drove home that night, I realized something: I had learned a lot. The pain of that experience produced some needed wisdom. In fact, truths had been revealed to me that I didn't even know existed. Nelson Mandela once said, *"I never lose a debate. Either I win, or I learn."*

One of the great tragedies of our time is that sizable segments of our population are now avoiding any truth that discomforts them. Liberals listen only to liberals. Conservatives listen only to conservatives. We even have our own news networks that shield us from all those facts that implicate our cherished opinions. When this happens, the culture becomes like an alcoholic family. It sweeps unpleasantries under a rug. It avoids, denies and deflects attention away from anything that burdens us with the responsibility to mature. Growth becomes impossible and we stay the same - year after year - because our lives are defined by scholastic laziness and an abandonment of integrity. What's worse, when people of faith discard unpleasant facts they are essentially discarding the God they claim to love. One of my teachers once asked a class of college freshman, *"If God is a God of truth, what are you afraid of? If you encounter some facts that hurt your pride, do you think God will change the truth so you don't have to grow in wisdom?"*

Dietrich Bonhoeffer put it another way: *"When Christ calls a man, he bids him come and die."*[16]

In Western countries, we have this thing called the "free marketplace of ideas". It suggests that if everyone is permitted

---

16   Dietrich Bonhoeffer, *The Cost of Discipleship* (London: Macmillan Publishing Company, 1963)

an opportunity to express an opinion without fear of political or criminal reprisal, the whole society benefits. After all, nobody has a monopoly on the truth. We all have something to offer and we all need to be tested. Most importantly, when a debate of ideas is permitted, falsehoods tend to be exposed for what they are, and truth tends to rise above the lies. This is why tyrants hate free speech. This is why they control the flow of information. This is why they see ignorance as a virtue. This is why a free press is viewed as an enemy.

A few months ago, I posted an essay on social media that dealt with a controversial topic. A few of my readers got angry with me and I lost their friendship. I was careful to speak as graciously as I could but it wasn't enough. To keep their friendship, I had to agree with them. At the same time, other readers disagreed with me but enjoyed the give-and-take. We respected each other. I think maturity enables a gracious sharing of different ideas so that we can all grow. Immaturity, on the other hand, runs away. It cherishes safety over learning and is easily offended. It dismisses people with words like 'fascist' and 'snowflake.' Ralph Waldo Emerson once wrote, *"Let me never fall into the vulgar mistake of dreaming that I am persecuted whenever I am contradicted."*[17]

A few years ago, an essay of mine went viral and I suddenly had an opportunity to speak with people in every corner of the globe. It gave me an opportunity to notice something about humanity. We grow up in isolated cloisters and we hear about strange cultures far beyond our borders. We think, "They aren't like us." Then something happens. Cancer strikes. A job is lost.

---

17   Ralph Waldo Emerson, Emerson in his Journals (Cambridge: Harvard University Press, 1982)

Death visits us. A lover betrays us. War invades our world. Our sense of security dissipates and suddenly... we are all the same. Their pain feels like our pain. Their teenagers act like our teenagers. Their culture respects humility. They want forgiveness too. They yearn to be dignified. We are essentially the same. It seems like such a simple idea but it is far from obvious when we remain isolated. In fact the fullness of our commonality jars us when we first discover it. But we all want to be safe. We all want to be valued. We all want our lives to have meaning. Those three desires are universal. They transcend culture, race, gender, faith and all the arbitrary boundaries we create. What divides us is the belief that other people don't matter as much as our people. What separates us is ignorance.

So how do we break down these walls? We do what tyrants and cowards don't want us to do. We speak with grace. We listen. We allow the truth to seep into our souls and transform us. It may be uncomfortable. It may be painful but there is no real LIFE without it. Cynthia Occelli[18] once said, *"For a seed to achieve its greatest expression, it must come completely undone. The shell cracks, its insides come out, and everything changes. To someone who doesn't understand growth, it would look like complete destruction."*

But that's the nature of a paradox. The joy we seek isn't possible without first experiencing the pain of our own inadequacies and allowing ourselves to "come undone"

> "Unless a seed falls to the ground and dies, it can bear no fruit."

---

[18] Cynthia Occelli author of *Resurrecting Venus* (Agape Media International, 2012)

PART THREE – BETRAYALS AND OTHER BLESSINGS

19

Surviving the Flying Monkeys

I became me when I was 55 years old. That was my age when I discovered who I was. The previous years seem blurry to me now - as if I had spent most of my life in a sack of amniotic fluid - unable to see beyond the womb and uncertain about the value I might eventually have. I owe much of my self-discovery to a few narcissists who made my life miserable and my awakening possible. Without them, and the people who believed their lies, I might never have wondered about things that truly mattered. It's been said that the two most important days of our lives are the day we were born and the day we discovered why.

It's odd how blind we can be when we live within a thicket of unhealthy people. The abnormal appears normal like a low grade fever that won't go away. At first we don't realize what's happening. Something might seem wrong but verbalizing our suspicions gets us into trouble. In a dysfunctional organization, the person who identifies the problem is punished while the person who causes it continues to operate with impunity.

I think anyone who has lived deep into adulthood has probably experienced a narcissist's venom. They are people who cannot examine themselves honestly, or feel empathy for their victims or express genuine remorse. They are also gifted at creating a culture of deceit where the truth is called a lie and a request for decency is punished with spite. Narcissists are also good at manipulating others to join their cause. The popular term for these enabling cohorts is "flying monkeys." They have their own reasons to participate in the process and their most effective weapon is slander whispered in secret.

A friend of mine recently described herself as "an empath in a hornet's nest of narcissists." That's exactly what it feels like - a hornet's nest. At first we don't have a clue about what's going on. My mom and dad were healthy, loving people and I grew up protected and naive. I had no idea what sort of wickedness awaited me as an adult. When we are unprepared for the 'hornet's nest', it's easy for a narcissist to make us doubt ourselves and question our own sanity. And with so many flying monkeys condemning our requests for honesty, who wouldn't be filled with doubt?

So... I'd like to offer some advice to those who find themselves abused by people who will never apologize for anything. I hope you find some comfort here...

> 1.) You are not who they say you are. Narcissists haven't earned the right to define you because they won't even examine themselves. The mere fact that they

have made you into their enemy speaks volumes about your integrity. You had the courage to speak when no one else did. Wear their condemnation as a badge of honor. They are attacking you because you discerned their deceits and named them. *"Truth does not mind being questioned. A lie does not like being challenged."*

2.) The fact that you were unable to fix the problem or reform the system or change anyone's heart, doesn't mean you failed. Your only task was to diagnose the illness. If they love their sickness more than your health, they failed, not you.

3.) Leave. Find some way to extricate yourself before every bit of life is sucked out of your soul. You owe it to yourself because that sick system is preventing you from bearing fruit and finding joy. You did your part and identified the problem, there is nothing more to do now. Sticking around will only intensify your abuse. If this sounds hopeless, it's because narcissists are constitutionally incapable of self-reflection and repentance. In their minds, their failures are always somebody else's fault. No one who loves their disease can be healed and unconditional love doesn't mean unconditional acceptance of bad behavior.

4.) This doesn't mean that everything is hopeless. YOU aren't hopeless. You are healthy. You desire truth. You love compassion. You want to grow. There is LIFE after you leave. The whole sick system with all its flying monkeys can be left behind and you can find joy again.

When I was in the 'hornet's nest' the only person who defended me died in the middle of the battle and I was left completely alone. That was the hardest part. I had to figure stuff out on my own. When we are being slandered in secret, a feeling of powerlessness overcomes us because we don't even know what's being said or who believes the lies. At one point I was forced to finally stop caring about what other people thought of me because there was nothing I could do about it anyway. One day I just screamed, "Screw everybody!" It was probably the most spiritual thing I could have said at the time. There is only one person in this universe that I want to please and I have no desire to please any narcissist with an entourage of flying monkeys.

Viktor Frankl, a man who survived a Nazi death camp and lost his family, wrote a book called, *Man's Search for Meaning*.[19] I pulled three quotes from his writings that mean a lot to me:

> *"To give light, one must first endure burning."*
>
> *"Man is that being who invented the gas chambers of Auschwitz but he is also that being who enters those chambers with the Lord's Prayer or the Shema Yisrael on his lips."*
>
> *"Everything can be taken from a man but one thing: the last of the human freedoms - to choose one's attitude in any given set of circumstances, to choose one's own way."*

---

[19] Victor Frankl, *Man's Search for Meaning* (New York: Pocket Books, 2006)

I chose decency. I chose to live among people who valued truth so that we could create a community defined by self-reflection, humility and growth. It will never be a perfect community but it is loving. You can find that joy too. There are gifts inside you yet to be discovered in a culture of affirmation and maturity. There are people who want you and who will appreciate your courage. You will be respected and cherished by those who know what you've endured. When you allow your wounds to be turned to wisdom, grateful people will receive you with loving arms.

20

The Ugly Silence

Sometimes we are 'loved' by people who have less than ordinary courage. It can be exasperating. I'm not talking about romantic love. I'm talking about any kind of brotherly or sisterly love that's wishy-washy and unaccompanied by a willingness to go out on a limb or stand up for what's right or defend you when you've been maligned. I don't like being 'loved' by wusses. I have a few bros who need to grow a pair.

There's something about love that requires sacrifice. It's not something that shows itself only when the risks are minimal. Real love is an all-in kind of thing.

It's also not just about loving individuals we know. It can be about doing justice. It can be about defending strangers who are being victimized. We don't have a right to silence or inaction if we claim to be people who walk with integrity. Love isn't cowardly. Love isn't cheap. Love takes risks. Love is inconvenient. Love compels righteousness. If it's not courageous, it's not love. Remove devotion from love and all you've got is a cuddly thing from the Dollar Store.

One evening in 1963, as my family sat around the dinner table, my dad posed a question to us: "What would you do if you were laying in bed one night and suddenly heard a woman being attacked on our front lawn?"

I was nine years old at the time but I remember vividly the dialogue that followed. It was a conversation about ethics and integrity and courage and how faith doesn't exist in a vacuum but rather in a world filled with nauseating cruelty and obligations to resist that cruelty.

My dad asked his question because a beautiful young woman had been murdered earlier that week in an affluent borough of NYC – not that far from our home on Long Island. Her name was Kitty Genovese. Her attacker stabbed her repeatedly while her screams echoed throughout the neighborhood. The police later determined that forty-three witnesses heard her cries for help. Forty-three witnesses turned on their lights and looked out their windows. Forty-three witnesses went back to bed without offering any help or calling the police. Forty-three witnesses later said, "I just didn't want to get involved."

In 1963, the Holocaust was still fresh in many minds and a Jewish editor of the New York Times latched onto this story because the plight of Kitty Genovese raised a fundamental question: "Why do seemingly good people do nothing and say nothing while the innocent are being brutalized?" What does it say about us as a nation when we are silent witnesses to something grotesquely immoral or when groups of people are demonized or when the powerful abuse the powerless with impunity?

Perhaps you know what it feels like to be abused. It is

painful enough to suffer that indignity but when no one comes to your aid, it's like being told that you are worthless. The silence of your 'friends' doesn't just feel like silence, does it? It feels more like contempt. It's as if someone is telling you:

> "I only want to love you when it's easy."
> "I don't believe you."
> "Justice and mercy don't interest me"
> "Neither does your safety."
> "I prefer to be shallow rather than deep."
> "Discernment is overrated."
> "I'm comfortable. Please don't disturb my ease."
> "You aren't worthy of a defense."

I'm convinced that integrity and righteousness are two vital components of love. Love is the willingness to stand up for someone or some ideal even when it's awkward or painful. When we fail to do this for even our own friends, we look more like strangers and the feelings of abandonment that this engenders can be completely demoralizing.

"*In the end, we will remember not the words of our enemies but the silence of our friends.*" Martin Luther King, Jr.

21

Their Finest Hour

Sometimes when I think about my past, I'm reminded of the stupid things I've done. A memory will come to me and suddenly I'll feel my face turning red and instinctively, I will wag my head at myself and my eyes will roll and I'll wish I could have a few "do-overs." I also wish I could say that my stupid decisions were mostly made in my youth but they weren't. My only excuse (if I have any at all) is that pain distorts everything and when we can't think clearly, we do dumb things and then we suffer the consequences.

I recently saw a post on social media that said, "To be old and wise, you must first be young and stupid." I guess once we suffer the consequences of our actions, we say, "I'm never going to do that again!" and that's how we acquire wisdom.

But what if we don't? What if we never examine ourselves honestly? What if we blame others for our mistakes? I think I may have mentioned this before but it's worth repeating: A healthy person isn't someone who never screws up. A healthy person is someone who screws up and says, "I screwed up.

Would you forgive me? How can I make this right? I'm sorry."

I have a friend who is a psychiatrist. One day she came for dinner and I asked her, "Why do some people find it impossible to admit anything? I don't understand it. If everyone else in this world was perfect and I was the only flawed person, I can see how it would be difficult for me to admit my mistakes. But everyone is flawed. We all screw up. Why is it so impossible for some individuals to take responsibility for their actions?"

My friend replied by saying that a narcissist might project an image of power and strength but inside, he is a frightened child who has an extremely fragile sense of self. If someone like that ever admitted a mistake, he would feel like he was saying, "I'm worthless" so he will never examine himself honestly, he will never confess anything and he will never allow himself to feel remorse.

All of this takes on deeper meaning during a time of crisis. As a pandemic forces us to self-isolate, we might be compelled to think about what truly matters and we begin focusing on things that heal and redeem us. It's also natural for us to use the vocabulary of warfare to describe the battles we fight. Now, as in World War 2, there are two theaters of action. One enemy is a virus that attacks the body and the other enemy is a virus that attacks the soul. The virus that attacks the soul thrives on deceit and ignorance. It is actually the more deadly contagion. The Coronavirus has no brain. It may wreak its havoc for a little while but it is no match for scientific ingenuity. After all, we are human beings equipped with minds that can decipher biological mysteries. Masks and ventilators can be produced, therapies will be developed, a vaccine can be discovered.

But the second virus has a brain. It is the most virulent of all pathologies. It is humanity's absurd capacity to engage in self-deceit and self-acquittal. It can be just as creative and ingenious as the most brilliant among us. It is constantly probing for weaknesses that it can exploit.

This is where real leadership becomes so necessary and inspirational. I'm in awe of people like Winston Churchill or Abraham Lincoln who faced-down enemies in the darkest of times. They were both brilliant at weaponizing the English language against diabolical forces. We can all learn something from them. In the early days of World War 2, when London was being fire-bombed almost nightly, Churchill did so much more than rally his troops. He rallied a civilian army and told them their victory was inevitable. With calm determination he never lied about the enemy's strength. He told the awful truth. He knew that failure would mean civilization would cease to exist and the world would be plunged into another Dark Age. He told his people that they would be redeemed from this evil by the power of righteousness and that every single soul in England would go down in history as a hero because they faced Hitler's onslaught with integrity and courage and that THIS would be Britain's finest hour.

We need leaders like Churchill today. We need people who value truth and scientific inquiry. We also need leaders who won't behave like narcissists - lying about their failures or sugar-coating the awful dangers we face.

We need to learn from our own mistakes as well. For many years, people in my country have called for "limited government" and have earnestly tried to gut the power of agencies designed to protect our environment, financial institutions, and public safety. Limited government works perfectly in a perfect world but we live in a world where corporations dump toxins in our drinking water, industrialists exploit the powerlessness of workers, hedge fund managers defraud investors, and uneducated thugs mock scientists who warned us of pandemic scourges. Now is not the time for narcissism. We need to repent of an economic theory that has left all of us unprotected.

A few days ago, I heard General McCrystal on television. He was asked what advice he would give to our leaders. He said, "Tell the truth." If a commander lies to his troops before a battle and he tells them that the enemy is a push-over, he will send his soldiers into battle psychologically unprepared for the carnage they will face. Those who survive will never trust that commanding officer again. "Truth is a real thing." It matters.

What shouldn't matter in times like these, are the terms "liberal" and "conservative." If we aren't vigilant, the two viruses will infect us all. We don't need polarizing figures on the left and right. We need healers in positions of power - people who know how to examine themselves honestly and who can treat everyone with dignity. If we don't gird ourselves with righteousness, and value the truth, civilization will cease. It is never appropriate to give a narcissist power. Not if he is liberal. Not if he is conservative. If we don't hold narcissists accountable for their daily deceits, we will be plunged into another Dark Age. But if we face the onslaught of these two viruses with courage and integrity, every single one of us will become heroes. It begins with humility and a willingness to learn from our mistakes but I am convinced that generations from now, people will look back at what we did and say, "This was their finest hour because they confronted two scourges and prevailed."

22

Love Letter to a Scapegoat

Dearest Friend,

    I've wanted to write some words of comfort to you because I know how long you've suffered and I want to acknowledge your battle and your courage. You are someone I respect deeply. Although at first you seemed uncertain about how to conduct yourself in such a toxic place, you eventually found your voice. You made difficult, but healthy decisions despite the intense loneliness you felt. Sometimes the moral choices we face in life aren't between good and evil. Sometimes we must choose between the lesser of two evils. I hate those times. No matter what we do, something awful will happen. But those choices are inevitable in a broken world.

    I know the deep sorrow you endured as you left loved ones because they wouldn't stop hurting you and could never apologize for anything. I have watched you grow since then and I want to affirm you. I have seen the fruit you've harvested.

You are now free to create, nurture, and love people who, like you, want to be whole. You are no longer fighting battles that could never be won. You are becoming the beautiful person you were meant to be.

There were times when you felt powerless - as if all your strength was drained from your soul. But you set boundaries anyway. Only a powerful person could do that. You walked away when you needed to. Your well-being, your witness, your fruitfulness were more important to you than any person's fragile ego. You reached a point in your life where you said, "Enough. I will no longer give anyone permission to harm me." There were those who were so adept at making you feel guilty for this choice but you spoke the truth, suffered the consequences, and moved on to a healthy place. You not only demonstrated courage, you modeled integrity. I love you for that. Your actions have been an inspiration to me even though they were accompanied by so much heartache and loss.

Whenever we confront a sick system we will be punished. This is true for families, religious institutions, corporations, and governments. Speaking truth to power has never been a safe endeavor. We will be accused of 'rocking the boat', rebelliousness, ingratitude, selfishness. They will make us question our own sanity and our worth. But we know what decency looks like and we know when it is absent. Its absence is like a hollow void in our souls.

Frederick Douglass once wrote, *"Those who profess to favor freedom and yet depreciate agitation, are people who want crops without ploughing the ground; they want rain without thunder and lightning; they want the ocean without* the roar of its many waters. *The struggle may be a moral one, or it may be a physical one, or it may be both. But it must be a struggle. Power concedes nothing without a demand; it never has and it never will."*

You made that demand and you met your responsibility. You did it when many others would have been silent. The results were not pretty. You were discarded as garbage. One of the hardest decisions we can ever make is to walk away from a loved one who insists on damaging us. The words, "Love never fails" echoes through our minds and we feel compelled to stay where we aren't wanted - hoping that our devotion will change a person's heart. But things only get worse.

I found a proverb that says, *"Do not reprove a scoffer, or he will hate you. Reprove a wise man and he will love you forever."*[20] There is so much wisdom in those words. I used to live with people who punished me when I spoke the truth. Now I live with people who beg me to speak it. Instead of fighting battles with those who have no desire to grow, we are bearing fruit. We are encouraging the broken-hearted. We are feeding our souls with joy. Like you, I am finding my place in this world. I could not have done this without examples like yours.

When you chose to be whole, you held a mirror up to your abusers and they hated you for it. They slandered you. They gaslighted you. They turned your 'friends' against you. But you stood firm. You would not allow anyone to suffocate you anymore.

But there was one more thing that you did that earned my deepest respect. You could have become cynical but instead

---

20   Proverbs 9:8

you went deep. You asked the hard questions: "How did this happen? How has it changed me? What lessons can I learn? Is it possible for all this pain to be redeemed so that I am transformed into a healer rather than a mere victim?" You became more and more empathetic and reflective. You now have a deep, redeeming perspective that informs your life and the lives you touch.

Last Spring I saw a double rainbow in my backyard. It was a gift to us as a reminder of the joy coming our way - especially now that our storms have passed. I would also like to leave you with one of my favorite quotes. It comes from the mind of an ancient Greek thinker named Aeschylus and I hope you treasure it and hold it close to you whenever you remember all the way you've come...

> "In our sleep, pain which cannot forget, falls drop by drop upon the heart until, in our own despair, against our will, comes wisdom through the awful grace of God."[21]

---

21   Aeschylus, Agamemnon l. 176

23
The Intifada of the Soul

I have a love/hate relationship with a word. Sometimes it's associated with pain. Other times, pure joy. But it always makes me think. The word is 'iconoclasm'.

Iconoclasm is that thing that asks us to question our stupid but cherished myths. It calls us to move outside of our comfort zones and think beyond our cloisters. It also requires a troubling amount of integrity and that's why it's so hard. To embrace iconoclasm, we have to explore terrifying places like the ugliest depths of our own depravity. It says, "What you call holy, might be profane" and it beckons us to release our white-knuckled grip on something that's destroying us.

A good example of iconoclasm is found in the following words...

> "You have heard it said, 'Love your neighbor and hate your enemy.' But I tell you, love your enemies

and pray for those who persecute you, so that you may be children of God."[22]

But... for years, I struggled with anger. I stayed to myself a lot because I was afraid it would spill out and everyone would see it. I told myself, "It's justified" although it was really a metastasizing cancer that wanted to eat me alive.

Sometimes I would wake up in the middle of the night to fight the battle yet again and I'd feel like a Palestinian fighter with a slingshot - facing down an army of tanks. I didn't care how impotent I was. I just wanted to vent my pain. I lived in that war zone and fought that battle for almost twenty years. It was a place of unjustified humiliation and abandonment - a place where I would scream my resentment alone so that no one would ever witness the shame I felt. The battle wasn't really against my enemies. It was more like an intifada of the soul - a struggle against myself - to forgive the unforgivable and to love what seemed impossible to love.

I didn't know how to do that. It was hard to let go of things. How do we forgive people who feel no remorse? Especially when the abuse is ongoing? I wanted to punish. I wanted to satisfy a desire for revenge. It felt like my cause was righteous, but I knew my secret responses were profane, futile and debilitating.

Occasionally, as I fought that battle in the dead of night, I would be distracted by my bedroom window. It would often frame a sight of infinite beauty. From that window I could see glimmering constellations that were far beyond my reach

---

22   Matthew 5:43-48

and light-years from my misery. I would get out of bed and sit on the floor - eyes transfixed on the splendor of it all. On a crisp winter's night, the moon and stars and planets would fill my universe with wonder - like a chorus of angels singing the same redeeming, iconoclastic song: "What you call holy, might be profane"

I kept seeing parallels between my own struggles to forgive and the struggles between Palestinians and Israelis.

Two words of wisdom were once offered on this matter of revenge and its futility. They stand as witnesses against both the darkness of our souls and the senselessness of the hatred:

> "Insanity is doing the same thing over and over again and expecting a different result." - -Albert Einstein

> "You become secure by doing justice and correcting oppression... so stop shedding innocent blood in this place."
> -Jeremiah

And yet we still cling to a foolish myth: "I will be satisfied when those who are unable to feel remorse suffer even more."

That is the myth we cherish so much - even though all of our anger has gotten us nowhere. The intifada of the soul is a struggle against the powers of darkness inside us all. They wish to dehumanize a person so that more land can be stolen, more walls can be built, more vengeance can be justified - as if all of THAT could ever make us safe or that doing it in the name of God can somehow turn the obscene into something sacred. It is the vilest myth ever created by broken humanity.

But occasionally, I catch glimpses of salvation. It is almost always framed in my bedroom window. There is something about being transported far above ourselves that puts things in perspective and jars us out of our stupidities. In the dead of night, when I sit on my bedroom floor and stare up at the infinite spectacles of time-warping space with its black holes and supernovas, I can't help feeling eclipsed by the wonder of it all. I am looking at stars whose light has traveled 186,000 miles per second for a billion years to reach my eyes. There is something redemptive about being humbled by a universe so immense and a Creator who offers us freedom from our turmoil. Humility is where the physical and spiritual realms make love. It's a place where we can remove the garments of our shame and arrive naked and contrite and yearning to be released from all the hatreds that define us. It is where we begin to see others as they are. Hurt people, hurting people and we begin to feel a transforming sense of sorrow.

I've also noticed that when we forgive, the world takes notice. It's so unnatural that it shocks the soul of every observer. The forgiver is seen as having a moral authority that is so rare and so desirable that people begin to think,

"Maybe this is the answer. Maybe this is the only answer."

When we see it in a moral leader, it is like sitting on a bedroom floor in the dead of night, listening to the voices of a celestial choir, "What you call holy, might be profane". It fills us with wonder and leaves us longing for more...

24

Forgiven

Last month I watched the first episode of 'Ted Lasso'. The show had earned some Emmys and I wanted to see what all the fuss was about. By the end of the week I had binge-watched the first two seasons. I guess I was hooked because it's such a deep and fascinating dive into the human condition. Every single character in that show is a contrast between power and fragility. There is a wealthy woman who was betrayed by her husband, a coach who lost his wife, a ridiculed 'nobody' who is finally treated with dignity but is unable to handle it, and an arrogant European football player whose father continually berates him. There are all these broken souls and each one holds some pain that we can easily identify with.

During one of the later episodes, a team psychiatrist makes a comment that really spoke to me. She said, *"The truth will set you free but first it will piss you off."*

In the previous chapter I spoke of my struggle to forgive. I've always presumed that forgiveness is something we offer to those who ask for it or who have expressed some empathy towards the people they've hurt. When I was young, I was taught that contrition precedes forgiveness. My heart always melts when I see a remorseful person and it's easy for me to forgive and move on after that. But giving grace to a spiteful person seemed impossible for me. Some people have told me that I should forgive just to release myself from the agony of the past. I didn't know how to do that. It's not like there's some switch that we just turn off and suddenly everything is rosy again. But after fighting this battle for so many years, I think I've finally figured out how and why to do it…

When I was in my 20s I had a friend I'll call 'Lydia'. She had a sweet disposition and was very likable. But one day she said something hurtful to another friend of mine and I wanted to talk to her about it. When I approached the topic, I could see her walls go up immediately. I suggested an apology might be helpful in repairing the rift between the two friends but what followed could only be described as 'volcanic.' I was standing in her apartment and a doorway stood between us. As soon as the word 'apology' left my lips, Lydia erupted and began screaming, "F-you! F-you! F-you! F-you!" She screamed it over and over and over again and each time she screamed it, she slammed the door in my face and then opened it so she could scream her next "F-you!" I had no idea what to do. I think I just stood there in shock with my mouth agape. I had grown up in New York public schools where 'cruel was cool' and obscenities were the norm but I had never witnessed the kind of rage that poured out of my friend that day.

Lydia used to tell me that she had a 'damaged brain' because of all the drugs and alcohol she consumed as a teenager.

But when the door finally slammed in my face for the last time, I collapsed into a chair and thought, "This isn't just a damaged brain. This is a deeply wounded soul."

Over the years, I have encountered several people like Lydia. They can appear safe and even endearing until someone says, "You hurt me" and then suddenly the anger and denial and spite gushes out. There have been times when I've been indignant over their inability to examine themselves honestly or to show even a little remorse for their behavior. They have such a fragile sense of self that they can't bear to acknowledge any harm they've caused. I guess it's just too painful for them. What I've finally realized is that it's not that they won't acknowledge it. It's that they CAN'T and for some sad reason, their conscience seems dead.

I finally had to accept the fact that asking such people to show remorse is like asking a person with two broken legs to run a marathon. I didn't want to believe that. But I had to. When we've been wronged, we want healing to take place. We want peace and order restored to our world. But sometimes, no matter how badly we might want it, it's not going to happen. We are asking for the impossible and once we realize that, pity seems to be the only appropriate response. At first, it's infuriating ("The truth will set you free but first it will piss you off"), but then it's liberating.

This doesn't mean that we have to stay in an abusive relationship. But once we've left and the dust has settled, it's better to view these broken people with compassion rather than resentment.

As I thought about my own vulnerability and the way I've responded to such people, two questions came into focus:

"Why do I care so much about the way wounded people treat me?" ...and (more importantly), "Upon what do I base my value?"

In her book, 'Edge of Wonder', Victoria Erickson writes, *"Transformation isn't sweet and bright. It is a dark and murky painful pushing - an unraveling of the untruths you've carried in your body - a practice in facing your own created demons - a complete uprooting before becoming."*[23]

One of the untruths that needed to be unraveled in my life was this crazy notion that my value was based on what other people thought of me. When broken people diminished me or mocked me, I took it too personally and didn't understand why it was happening. It made forgiveness harder. But when I look back, I'm reminded that some of the most beautiful and respected figures in human history were brutalized by damaged people who lived in darkness. If anything, the courage and perseverance of our heroes endeared them to us all the more. They were able to stand against the storm without questioning their own value because they knew that their worth and their purpose was based on something greater than their abusers' opinions. Indeed, it was based on something of eternal significance. After all these years, I've decided that I want to be like those heroes of history because theirs is the knowing that makes forgiveness and freedom possible.

---

23   Victoria Erickson, *Edge of Wonder* (Acton, Ontario: Enrealment Press, 2015)

25

Epiphanies

When my parents were born in the early decades of the twentieth century, astronomers thought our galaxy was the entire universe. Over time, our understanding changed. Ten years ago, we were told 100 billion galaxies filled the cosmos. More recently, that estimate became 200 billion. Then, only a few months ago, the scientific consensus was altered again. The James Webb telescope parked itself a million miles from earth and began sending back images of the universe that dazzled everyone.

The telescope had a different kind of lens. It saw infrared light rather than the usual spectrum seen by the human eye. The lens was pointed at a small patch of darkness. What happened next was described by NASA as a spiritual experience. Myriads of galaxies appeared. Some were billions of light years away. Suddenly, we were able to peer back in time to almost the beginning of everything. What was once thought to be nothing was filled with immeasurable glory and astronomers now believe the universe contains trillions of galaxies. In just one human lifetime, our entire understanding of everything has been transformed.

Seeing light in darkened spaces has always been a spiritual experience - especially when everyone else presumed there was nothing there. I know tender souls who have spent their entire lives being devalued and demeaned. Often a culture will lack the ability to see beyond the spectrum of its own biases. We live in a world that asks, "Can anything good come from Nazareth?" because it presumes that a land of half-breeds and misfits could never produce anything of glory.

I have a dear friend who finds it difficult to get medical care because she lives in a country that discriminates against anyone who has the wrong surname or who grew up in a place called 'Mosquito Hollow.' Her world says that her skin isn't light enough, her body isn't thin enough, her car isn't fancy enough. She is intelligent, disciplined and hardworking to the point of exhaustion. She has earned two degrees and is constantly trying to better herself but everyday the world reminds her that she will never be good enough.

There are also times when she feels shame despite all of her hard work. I was speaking to her recently and I suggested that there are two kinds of shame. There is the shame we feel when we make a mistake or a poor decision. But there is also unjustified shame. It is the shame we feel when we are demeaned or forsaken. It is like being convicted of a crime that we didn't commit. At those times, it seems like the whole world wants to believe a lie and we are left with no one to defend us or believe in us.

So how do we speak to a system that isn't seeing something of incredible value? A different kind of vision is required. It takes a spiritual telescope to find glory in darkened spaces. It takes a different kind of lens to see what others have written off.

Very often, when we direct a loving gaze at people who have been devalued and ignored, we not only discover hidden wonders, but we also come face to face with the terrible reality of our own subjectivity. When this happens and the scales fall from our eyes, we begin to question many of our previous assumptions. In a moment of epiphany, we escape our parochialism. We are free to think, free to point our telescopes at other dark, misunderstood places, free to glory in all the unexpected light that we find there and free to love those who have been disinherited by the kingdoms of this world.

I'm reminded of a passage in the book of Job. Job had been asked a multitude of unanswerable questions. When he realized he had no answers, he let go of his pride and his indignation and acknowledged how blind he had been. He saw the arrogance of his previous assumptions and confessed these words, "I spoke of things that I did not understand, things that were too beyond me to even know. I'm sorry. Please forgive me."

To those who have spent too many years being devalued and written off, I want you to know that your shame is unjustified. You have been convicted by a kangaroo court. There are wonders inside you that can easily be seen by people who own a spiritual lens. Seek out people like that. Listen to their voices and not the others. Your hurtful experiences and humiliations have produced a value system within you that puts your accusers to shame. Your pain has given you an extraordinary beauty that many of us long to see. You are defined by humility, compassion and grace. Those things are priceless in the Kingdom of God which, even now, is breaking in among us because of you.

26

Finding Home

Yesterday I planted a flower garden. I bought special soil from a guy who advertises it as "The best poop in the valley." It's basically dirt mixed with cow poop, chicken poop, and pig poop. I've purchased the stuff before and can attest to its miraculous ability to propagate perennials. So after planting lilies, foxgloves, irises, lilacs, and hollyhocks, I mulched it and sat down to admire the whole thing. My garden wasn't even an hour old when the butterflies and hummingbirds discovered it. I don't know how they found it so fast but I like to think that beauty attracts beauty.

It's funny how something as unappealing as poop can produce so much joy. When I first started gardening, I didn't know about the stuff. I think I was in my twenties when I put some tomato plants in disappointing soil. I grew a bumper crop of weeds that summer and gave up gardening for the next thirty years.

Lately I've realized that people with relationship problems face the same questions as gardeners: "Do I really want to invest a lot of time in soil that only grows weeds? What do I do with all the poop people put in my life? Do I just get angry or can I cultivate something amazing with it?"

Sometimes people behave poorly towards us. Their fragile egos and frail personalities testify to the emptiness in their souls and they can't stop damaging others. It's like cow poop, chicken poop and pig poop all mixed together and you have to know what to do with it.

I went through a period where I felt obligated to stay with people who couldn't learn from their mistakes. The same hurtful behaviors were repeated over and over again and no one was willing to examine themselves honestly. When I finally woke up to the futility of being with them, I decided to do something special. I sold my house, bought some land in the mountains and built a new home far away from their cruelty. I framed-up my house in two months - eager to prove to the world that I wasn't old and decrepit yet. It was good therapy after so many demoralizing losses. I felt so free and happy and as I began my new life, I discovered something. We tend to think of redemption as a purely spiritual thing. But I could actually see it and touch it as my life was being rebuilt with new priorities and goals. I began to surround myself with loving people and I felt valued. I'm not fighting stupid battles anymore. My energy is going into the lives of loved ones who are grateful and honest.

I'm also enjoying the fresh mountain air and changing seasons and breathing in joy everyday. My natural neighbors are wild turkeys, deer, fox, black bears and an occasional moose. They're all very civil except for the fox. Last evening, as the sun was sinking, I sat quietly on a lawn chair at the edge of the woods. The fox stopped by for a visit. He had a big red tail as long as his body and the little philistine didn't even notice my beautiful new garden. He just sniffed the ground - looking for voles and then walked away unimpressed. I rolled my eyes and thought, "That dude's taste is all on his tongue." But he's the only one who seems aloof around here. Everyone else has been really sweet.

So here's the thing... infidelity and betrayal can be life-changing events. When we first experience it, it smells like poop. If we aren't careful, it can create a kind of sepsis in our souls that leads to bitterness and rage. But if we ask the right questions, pain can lead to a deeper understanding of ourselves and healing can result. You'd never think something that smells like poop could produce anything good in our lives. But if we take the time to process the anguish and learn something deep and transformative, those lessons will begin to saturate and fertilize what might once have been an arid wasteland. The rain falls and seedlings begin to sprout and miraculous things happen. We will begin attracting people into our lives who know how to love because beauty is drawn to beauty. It's like butterflies and hummingbirds finding a brand new garden. We can learn a lot from them because they know where the nutrients are.

PART FOUR – LIFE AFTER LOSS

27

Awakening

There's a saying that's been floating around the internet for some time. I think it was first offered by Tony Robbins but it goes something like this: *"Change happens when the pain of staying the same is greater than the pain of change."*

I agree with that statement but I wish it wasn't true. I wish pain was unnecessary. I like being comfortable. But I'm also aware of how redemptive a painful process can be. I have seen it over and over again in the lives of people I love. I would like to share a few of their joyful experiences here but first, it might be helpful to suggest why 'comfort' can be one of the most depressing things in the world...

I have loved ones who are living under a veil of darkness. They see the world only as a conflict between left and right. They are eager to distort the character of the opposition and are blind to the shortcomings of their allies. They have dug in their heels and embraced principles and personalities that are full of deceit. I have known these loved ones for decades. They are good people who have lost their way. They are now rationalizing levels of depravity that would have once shocked their own collective conscience. But now, speaking to them is like speaking to cult members. No amount of pleading, reasoning, fact-checking or even LOVE will wake them from their darkness. They reside in a place where decency is no longer persuasive and they are comfortable with it all.

I began asking myself, "What has to happen before the veil can be lifted? The answer is always the same: When the pain of standing still exceeds the pain of moving forward, redemption happens. I wish it was easier. But the awful truth is that we first have to be willing to see what we've become before any growth is possible. A friend of mine recently posted these words on social media: *"You can't talk butterfly language to caterpillar people."*

A few years ago a church in the Midwest offered the following thoughts...

> *"The crucible of transformation often comes on the heels of loss, failure, or regret. It comes when we experience the pain of being forced to accept a reality that we can't change, or the consequences of choices that can't be undone. And this is the sobering, sacred space where we must choose life or death. Healing or resentment. Hope or despair. God always invites us to deeper hope through the practice of surrender."*[24]

That 'surrender' isn't about humiliation and defeat. It's about letting go of all the silly notions that hold us back. It's

---
24 Willow Creek Community Church, South Barrington, Illinois

about giving up our false securities and grabbing onto something solid and worthy of devotion.

I mention these things because the whole world is in crisis now. It's a good time to rethink our priorities. Every single one of us is facing a similar threat. Hundreds of thousands have died a needless death. It's also a world of knees on necks and messed-up priorities and worthless idols and kids in cages and military stockpiles that could incinerate everyone a thousand times over. Everywhere we look we see this strange combination of alienation and self-satisfaction without even realizing that those two attributes are the reason we are hurting.

All this sounds quite depressing but I've witnessed redemption too. I have seen people change. I know first hand how the pain of facing our fears, weaknesses, and traumas can lead to something beautiful.

I've been communicating with a young woman in Pakistan who experienced a painful event several years ago. We've been talking about how a person can discover herself after a time of grief and trauma. Lately I've noticed that she seems to have found her voice and come alive with courage and purpose - precisely because she's done the hard work of asking difficult questions and searching diligently for the answers. She still struggles with things but I can sense power in her. She is able to speak her mind and insist on things that matter. I love that about her. If I was her father I would feel blessed because she has become brave, honest, powerful and real.

Over time, my Pakistani friend and I have noticed that pain invites us into a time of reflection. It can deepen and mature us like nothing else. It can also expose the false securities that we've relied on for so long. I recently told her about a young girl in the US who was molested by a family member. One day her counselor asked her how she was feeling and the girl replied, "I'm fine as long as I don't wear my red dress." The little girl attributed her abuse to that beautiful red dress and she convinced herself that she would be safe if she just wore something else. We are all like that little girl. We cloak ourselves in things that cannot save and it takes time for us to realize that the only way to truly heal is to face our fears and traumas.

I have another friend whose husband betrayed her. After years of devotion she was replaced by another woman and was left to process her anguish alone. For a few years she spiraled down into an abyss of self-doubt and anger but she eventually found herself. She has a lot of personal integrity. She decided to listen to those who cherished her and affirmed her. She took an inventory of her creative talents and reinvented herself. She saw some people succeeding and she said, "I can do that." She went back to school and graduated and started a thriving business. All of that self-discovery and joy would probably never have been hers without the agony that began it and the introspection that followed. There is redemption in even the darkest places.

There is another young person I love. She lives in Africa. She recently asked me to be her 'Spirit Dad.' Her father had emotionally abandoned her years ago. Her mother witnessed the Rwandan genocide and turned to alcohol to dull the pain. Sometimes my African "Spirit Daughter' is awakened at night by her mother beating her. She lives in a country that offers no protection. She is educated and intelligent and we talk everyday about the things that enable growth. When I first met her, she was understandably sad. But she also has a fun-loving side to her. She says "coolbeans," a lot. I decided to call her 'Binti Coolbeans' because 'binti' is the Swahili word for 'daughter.'

Binti Coolbeans is rising above her circumstances too. Although she has borne the brunt of her parents' poor choices, she still has the courage to stand her ground. If she identifies the problem, she is mocked and ridiculed by her family but she persists in her quest for decency. I recently sent her two quotes. The first was from Denzel Washington: *"Your own family will talk bad about you when you are in the process of breaking all their generational curses. This ain't for the weak."*

The second quote was a gift from 'Anonymous.' It said, *"Never underestimate a cycle breaker. Not only did she experience years of generational trauma, but she stood in the face of that trauma and said, 'This ends with me.' This is brave. This is powerful. This comes at significant cost. Never underestimate a cycle breaker."*

Binti Coolbeans recently told me about a journey she took to a rural part of Africa. She had organized a trip to a rescue center for young girls who had escaped female genital mutilation. The girls shared their stories with her but they were also shy and scared because their male teachers were present. The men were asked to leave the room and the girls opened up about how the men were 'doing bad things to them.' The girls didn't even know that rape was a crime. Then they shared their stories about how their families had betrayed them. Some of the girls cried and said that this was the first time in their lives that someone had listened to them.

That experience was transformative for my binti.

Afterwards some of the girls hugged her and told her that she was an inspiration. For the first time in their lives they began to believe that they could rise above their circumstances. It was then that my African daughter decided to use her law degrees to help the most vulnerable.

This is why I love people who are wounded but searching for meaning. They have more power than they know.

Trauma often causes us to ask those ultimate questions in life: "Who am I? Why am I here? Where am I going?" The idea that pain deepens us is something that I love and hate at the same time. I wish there was another way but I don't think there is.

The process of change is often disruptive and sometimes even violent. Those who love a sick status quo will hate the truth and anyone who speaks it. Those who diagnose the problem accurately will be dismissed at best and demonized at worst. Those who speak out against the sickness will often enter a period of spiritual homelessness. It can engulf the soul like a swarm of locusts. Sometimes it feels like we can't even breathe. At those times, it's important to question the things we cling to and the false securities that offered us nothing. It's important to look for something deeper and authentic because redemption happens when the pain of standing still exceeds the pain of moving forward.

Each of the stories I've cited above have a common theme. There is something strangely beautiful about ugliness. Pain and heartache have a way of awakening the soul so that we see our lives in an entirely new way. This is when transformation happens. The darkness doesn't have to define us forever. We can be redeemed.

28

Penniless Wealth and Perilous Joy

In 1983, I was given a one-year research fellowship at Yale University. It was one of those deals where I had free access to the curriculum but I had to pay for my own room and board. My son, Justin, was only two years old and his mom was pregnant with our second son, Nathaniel. As soon as we moved there, we got a miserable dose of reality. Southern Connecticut is an expensive place to live. The only housing we could find was an uninsulated beach house on the Long Island Sound. The place was freezing in winter and we were always afraid to do our laundry because the water bill was outrageous. We had medical expenses related to the pregnancy as well as heat bills, car bills and grocery bills so... I took a job building condominiums four days per week. I managed to do my academic work on the other three days.

Despite my best efforts, we still weren't able to pay all the bills so one day we decided to sell an antique cupboard that was purchased on our honeymoon. It had a lot of sentimental value to us but we were broke so we called an antique dealer and asked him to stop at the house to check-out our treasure.

When the dealer arrived, we liked him right away. He was a kindly old man and when he saw the cupboard he said, "That's a beautiful piece! Why are you selling it?" I was a little embarrassed and joked self-consciously, "We's just po' folk. We need the cash."

The old man looked at us. Then he shook his head and said, "You're not poor. You just don't have any money."

His comment caught me off guard. It was so full of wisdom that I was left without words. After he bought the cupboard and left, I began to realize that I had never been poor - not even for one minute of my life. I think real poverty is about hopelessness and I had never been without hope. Whenever I imagined my future, I always pictured myself succeeding in something. I had no idea how I would succeed. But I knew I would.

Lately I'm been putting three women in Jamaica through college. They live in an impoverished area and have no running water in their home. They collect rain water from their roof. Their diet is plantains, vegetables and an occasional chicken. There are three sisters in the family and one of them has already earned a degree and acquired her first professional job. It's a big deal in Jamaica to have secure employment. Her sisters are also excited about their future because they finally have an opportunity to rise above their circumstances. I was speaking to them recently and told them my story of the kindly old man who taught me the real meaning of poverty. Remarkably, they said, "We have never been poor either."

When I was in Latin America, I saw some things. There were girls who were only nine or ten years old, living in extreme poverty. They would prostitute themselves to garbage truck drivers in exchange for the food scraps in the truck. They knew certain garbage trucks came from the restaurant district of the city and they could get some fairly fresh food if they had access to those trucks. So they sold their bodies for trash.

Ever since then, a certain question has been following me everywhere I go: *How do I live out my faith in a world where nine year old girls sell their bodies for trash?*

I recently learned of a millionaire in Florida who owns a lot of hotels. One day he decided to give free college educations to anyone living in an impoverished town near him. After he made that offer, the crime rate was cut in half and the high school graduation rate jumped from 25% to nearly 100%. Later, he said, "I just gave them hope. If you don't have hope, what's the point?"

Giving hope can sometimes be an act of faith - especially if we think we can't afford to do it. Most of us don't own hotels. We aren't millionaires. We have our own problems. A few weeks ago, I heard about a young woman whose father had abandoned her family right before her final year of college. As a result, she couldn't complete her studies and would have to take a menial job to support herself. When I heard about it, I thought, "I can't help her."

But I have this annoying faith. At inconvenient times it speaks absurdities and jars me from a mundane life. It says, "There is such a thing as penniless wealth and perilous joy, and believing in One who says, 'You can't, but I can. Do you trust me?'"

So I told that young woman to register for her final year of college and I sent a down payment. I've been an artist for almost forty years and have never had a steady paycheck. Somehow my needs have always been met so I stopped worrying about myself long ago. I still get surprised, though. This past month, as all the tuition bills were coming due, I was suddenly flooded with sales and orders. People started calling me from California, Missouri, Georgia, and Pennsylvania. It was like fishing on a lake all night long and catching nothing and then some miracle worker stops by and says, "Cast your net one more time." The next thing I know, my boat is swamped with fish and three years of tuition is paid for in less than a month.

A few years ago, during a sad time in my life, I decided to do some hiking in the Canadian Rockies. I knew there were creatures bigger than me in the surrounding woods. The real estate was owned by grizzly bears and wolves and I was clearly trespassing. There is something about being completely alone in wild places that causes our senses to be hyper-vigilant. The danger forces us to see and hear so much more than when we're in safer territory. It's actually exhilarating because we aren't just aware of the risks. We are aware of everything - the rustle of leaves, the trumpeting of elk, the towering peaks, the pristine waters, the awesome grandeur of life. A heightened sense of expectation dazzles the soul with a strange combination of heart-stopping trepidation and adrenaline-fueled ecstasy. It's like living on the edge and feeling cradled in serenity at the same time. It makes no sense but that's the way it feels.

The same is true when we take a leap of faith that seems unaffordable. Somehow we know that our souls can only be fed in untamed wildernesses and so the promise of joy overcomes the fear. That challenge is a gift that's offered to each of us. Maybe it's because we live in a world where little girls sell their bodies for trash. But one thing is certain: hope is a priceless thing and life can be so full of meaning...

29

Treasures

A few years ago, I found myself stuffed into the back of a pickup truck with fourteen other people as we drove through a garbage dump in Latin America. Teenagers were hanging onto all sides of the truck and the horn was beeping feverishly as waves of laughing children ran behind us. Everyone was excited because we were heading to an outdoor feeding area with chicken and rice and beans. When we got there, I took a photo of two barefoot sisters who had come for a meal. They lived in the dump with all the other kids. Their homes were made of sticks and sheets of plastic and corrugated tin. I didn't know how to speak to those two little girls because my Spanish was so poor but I sensed I was in the presence of something extraordinary - maybe even holy - as if God could appeared in human form, shoeless and draped in awkward clothes and priceless beyond belief.

Before I say more, I want to suggest a stunning fact: Every person reading these words is wealthier than Steven Jobs. Prosperity, as the world defines it, can give us an illusion of wealth but that's all it is - an illusion. One malignant lump on a billionaire's pancreas can terminate everything. The truth is, if 'security' is being able to save ourselves from any disaster, none of us will ever be secure - no matter how much money we have.

So I would like to propose a radical idea. It grew out of a question that's fascinated me for years. What is wealth? If money isn't accomplishing something - if it's just sitting somewhere, can we really call it valuable? Even if it's growing at a high rate of interest, does it have worth if something meaningful isn't being done with it? What if the fundamental purpose of wealth is to lift people up? ...and storing it away, devalues it? What would our lives look like, and what joy might we experience if we redefined our notion of 'treasure?'

I think we can clarify our purpose in life by distinguishing between "meaningless wealth" and "meaningful wealth" but it's not something many cultures encourage us to do. Forbes magazine publishes its annual list of the world's wealthiest people as if the existence of billionaires is an awe-inspiring thing but no consideration of how their wealth is used ever enters into the calculus. Money is glorified simply for being money - as if it has its own intrinsic awesomeness and yet some of the most miserable people I've known are trust fund babies with no sense of purpose. Solomon once wrote, *"Where there is no vision, the people perish."* I've also noticed that both ends of the political spectrum are seduced by the same lie about wealth. It doesn't matter if someone is a liberal junk bond king or a conservative prosperity gospel preacher. They have both embraced a distorted understanding of wealth. Spiritual poverty has a way of disfiguring everything.

Plato once said, *"Those who are able to see beyond the shadows and lies of their culture will never be understood, let alone believed, by the masses"* ...but I want to believe that even the masses can be transformed - especially during times of crisis - as we reevaluate our priorities and become who we were always meant to be. The thing is, we can be enslaved without even knowing it. Sometimes we are in denial of our own addictions. Someone once told me that if you throw a frog into boiling water it will jump right out but if you put a frog in lukewarm water and gradually turn up the heat, you can lull the frog to sleep and boil it to death. Sometimes I think our cultures are lulling us to sleep and boiling us to death by a slow, methodical attempt to indoctrinate us into a belief that says, "Money is everything". Harriet Tubman famously said, *"I freed a thousand slaves. I could have freed a thousand more if they only knew they were slaves."*

So what is the answer? ...and what kind of paradigm-shifting earthquake beneath our feet could cause us to completely redefine the nature of wealth? The universe might be 13.8 billion years old but in a deeply personal sense, it's just beginning because every time a crisis occurs, the Lover of our Souls invites us into a new creation where the real treasure we seek is two shoeless sisters living in a garbage dump or some other mission that gives us a renewed sense of purpose. There is always meaning in trauma. There is always purpose in crisis. Recently, a Big Bang has come into our lives in the form of a pandemic and it has the power to explode our subjectivities and vaporize our previous notions of wealth so that we can take part in something redemptive. These traumas come into our lives so that we don't get lulled to sleep and boiled to death. No doubt, other Big Bangs will follow but the beautiful paradox of it all is that if we are willing to be part of this new creation, the violence of these cataclysms can actually lead to joy.

30

Consider the Birds

A friend of mine is facing homelessness. She has worked hard all her life but she is a single mom and her son is severely disabled. His autism has recently been accompanied by seizures and loud screaming. It has become impossible to find childcare. Without someone to watch her son, she is unable to work. She feels like she's in a hopeless game of chess. Her savings have been exhausted. The rent is due soon. Checkmate is in two weeks.

Those of us who have lived through similar circumstances will never forget the terror of those days. They test our faith and deepen our yearnings. Very often the fear is accompanied by a sense of abandonment and shame. There have been several times in my life when I found myself alone and unable to produce a solution to the problems I faced. I have been a self-employed artist for years. I've never known from week-to-week where my next pay check was coming from. At first it was unnerving. But as the years unfolded, I realized that I had never been orphaned by the Lover of my soul. Very often "redemption" came at the eleventh hour - as if I was supposed to learn something significant during that time of testing. Certain words have been burned into my soul: *"You shall show mercy on the stranger for you were once destitute in a foreign land."*

I remember the only time I faced hunger. I was 22 years old. It was during a recession with high unemployment, high inflation, high interest rates and long lines at the gas pump. I had a car that kept breaking down and the only work I could find was a few odd jobs as a carpenter or painter. During the winter, I would shovel people's driveways. I rented a room from an elderly lady for $10/week. Her name was Annie Naylor. I remember she was very British. She kept a portrait of the queen in her living room and without saying a single word, she let it be known that people like me shouldn't socialize with people like her. My room had a bed, a desk and a closet for clothes. I put a tiny refrigerator in that closet and a little toaster oven sat on top of the refrigerator. My clothes always smelled like the food I cooked in the toaster the night before.

One day I woke up without anything to eat. I had a small job that would net me $40 that day so I figured I could pick up some food on my way home. I drove to the job site, completed my work and received the $40. But when I went to my car, I saw that one of my tires was flat. I tried my best to get the lug nuts off but they were frozen onto the wheel and I couldn't budge them. I was forced to call a tow truck so that the tire could be changed with a pneumatic wrench. The fee was $40.

As I drove home that day, I realized it would be the first

time in my life that I would go to bed hungry. No one knew what I was going through. I was too ashamed to tell anyone. When I arrived in my room, I sat at my desk with my head in my hands. I thought about praying but I didn't feel like it. After a while I grabbed a book on the desk, opened it half-heartedly to any page, and began to read...

> "Consider the birds of the air, for they neither sow nor reap nor gather into barns; yet your heavenly Father feeds them. ...and why do you worry about clothing? Consider the lilies of the field, how they grow: they neither toil nor spin; and yet I say to you that even Solomon in all his glory was not arrayed like one of these. Now if God so clothes the grass of the field, which today is, and tomorrow is thrown into the oven, will He not much more clothe you? Therefore do not worry, saying, 'What shall we eat?' or 'What shall we drink?' or 'What shall we wear?' For your heavenly Father knows that you need all these things. But seek first the kingdom of God and His righteousness, and all these things shall be added to you."[25]

Just then, there was a knock at my bedroom door. It was Annie Naylor. She was holding a tray with a complete dinner. There was chicken and mashed potatoes and green beans and a slice of apple pie. She had never done anything like this before and she had no way of knowing what had happened to me that day. She just said, "I was planning on having some

---

25   Matthew 6:26-33

guests tonight but they couldn't make it. Would you like some dinner?"

My life has been filled with experiences like this. They begin with misery and end with indescribable joy. These are the moments that feed our souls and not just our bellies. They compel us to ask the important questions in life: What does it mean to seek the Kingdom of God? Is there something inherently redemptive and transformative about suffering? Am I here to serve only myself? ...or is real joy hidden in the depths of another broken soul who longs to be cherished and loved so that she never has to hear the words, "checkmate"?

31

Beautiful

During my teenage years, I was an awkward geek. I was skinny and I sucked at sports and I had zits. I also had a beautiful twin sister. When we went to school, people would look at the two of us and ask me, "What happened to you?" So I liked to stay home a lot and think about things that mattered. It was painful to be devalued and dismissed during those early years. Later, when I was in my 20s I married a woman who was attractive and people would say, "How'd you get her?" It's strange how the humiliations of our youth can stay with us for decades and color the way we view ourselves. Even now, when people give me compliments, it's hard for me to believe them and I continue to be bothered that society expects greater things from beautiful people without considering the content of their character.

There's a famous study that observed the reaction of babies when pairs of faces were shown to them on a TV. The babies would stare at beautiful faces and ignore plain faces as if they were hard-wired to value external beauty. There are other studies that show how attractive people are offered higher salaries or given greater responsibilities even when their resumes wouldn't justify the privileges they received.

I'm writing about this now because recently a friend of mine experienced something painful. She lives in a developing country and has experienced a lot of hardship in her short life. But she also has the sweetest soul. My friend just started her third year of college and after her dorm room was paid for, she drove to the school to move in for the semester. When she arrived, the dorm manager informed her that there had been a 'mistake' and someone else was 'accidentally' given her room. She was told that she would have to accept a smaller room in the corner.

No one could understand how the mistake was made. She had paid for the same room she lived in during the previous year. The manager had guaranteed the room. She also bought curtains that fit the windows and now they were unusable in the smaller space.

The next morning, as she was leaving, she looked down the hallway and noticed a white woman leaving her old room. She immediately realized what had happened. The shocking thing is that the culture is predominantly black and the manager was black too. So when I heard what had happened, I asked my friend how could this occur in a country where nearly everyone is of African descent? I was told, "Will, this is the way it has always been. This is why black people bleach their skin. The whole culture gives preferences to anyone with lighter skin. It's all so arbitrary."

My faith tells me that the priorities of God are different than those of this world. We look at physical faces but God looks at the heart. The more humble and tender and tested we are, the more beautiful our spirits become. There is something so attractive about a counter-cultural movement that rejects the values of a fallen world and offers something liberating instead.

The thing is, my friend is beautiful on the inside and the outside. Her life is an inspiration to me. When she was 11 years old and wasting away from terminal cancer, the hospital sent her home to die. She prevailed against all odds for reasons unknown but she is full of courage and faith. This is what beauty looks like. She is sweet and she walks with dignity. I want to be like her. There is something so foolish about an ethic that dismisses and devalues a young woman arbitrarily without even considering the glory in her soul. The kingdom of God doesn't look like the kingdoms of men. It is a place where the first are last and the last are first. It wants to break into a world full of diminished souls and oppressive regimes and turn it right side up. If our faith isn't exposing and confronting the cruelties of this world, it's not doing what it's supposed to do.

So I've been dreaming... In this life, our bodies are subject to the laws of physics and eventually will go the way of all flesh. But what of our spirits? They aren't affected by entropy and decay. What if everyone reading these words could meet seven centuries from now? What would we see in each other after our bodies have been discarded? Could we fly away to a place where every mountain is laid low and every valley lifted up and all the crooked paths made straight? What would beauty look like then and what are the implications for how we live our lives now? Would the beauty we have there be the beauty we cultivate here? Humility, mercy, generosity, wisdom ...Would those be the things we see when we look upon each other in the age to come?

32

Beacons in a Darkened Space

I have a favorite question. I pose it to myself often and to people who find themselves at one of life's intersections where important decisions are made. It's a question that has a way of centering all of us...

"What is the deepest longing of your heart?"

The amazing thing is that everyone I know answers the question in a similar way:

"I want to be cherished by someone deeply and I want my life to be full of meaning."

It's strange how one single question has a way of revealing humanity's common hope. It doesn't matter if we are rich or poor, male or female, black or white. It doesn't matter if we have a faith or if we lost one or if we never had one. Every single one of us seems to emerge from our mother's womb with a deep yearning to be cherished and, as we mature, we want our lives to matter.

I also like the question because it has a way of dignifying people. When we ask it of someone, we are essentially saying, "I want to know you more fully because you are precious to me." Sometimes people think of their inadequacies and wonder if they're worthy of *anything*, but simply asking the question suggests that being lovable doesn't have anything to do with power or perfection. Often, the most vulnerable people are also the most tender and sweet and adorable. In fact, our inadequacies are the very things that prepare us for intimacy and redemption.

A few years ago, my youngest daughter and I were in Sequoia National Park. We had spent the morning driving to some high elevations and when we got to about 5,000 feet we found a small lake with beaches and a campground. Emily and I had always enjoyed competing so we challenged each other to a swim race across the lake. I was 52 years old and Emily was 16. I knew she would kick my butt but I couldn't resist the competition. So we both dove in and were racing across the water at break-neck speed until I got to the middle of the lake and realized I was having a hard time breathing. I thought it was my age. When I was younger, I ran marathons and swam a lot and I had never experienced the sensation of too little air in my lungs.

But now, I was in the middle of a lake with nothing to grab onto and I felt exhausted. Emily had already zoomed past me and was unaware of the trouble I was in. I later realized it was the thin air at the high elevation that caused the problem. But at the time, I just thought I was getting old and should have known better than to race a 16 year old girl across a lake. So I flipped over on my back and decided to float there until I could catch my breath. It didn't work. I continued to have a hard time filling my lungs. I remember the feeling of total helplessness and wishing there was something to hold on to. I called for help but I was too far from shore for anyone to hear and I began to think I might not survive this.

So I drifted like a leaf on the water for what seemed like an eternity. Finally, someone saw me struggling and swam out to me with an inner tube. I heard the splashing of an approaching swimmer and when I turned my head, I saw that big black inner tube floating next to me and was overcome with joy. As soon as I grabbed onto it, I knew I was going to live.

Being vulnerable isn't necessarily a bad thing. It's scary but it's also liberating. It frees us to tap into powers greater than ourselves. The arrogant aren't interested in such things. They say, "I don't need anybody." But people who have been humbled by life can accomplish so much more because they've learned about their weaknesses and have grabbed on to something bigger.

I also discovered a wonderful truth about us: *Making mistakes is how we get to be awesome.* Maturity is what happens when we are humbled, not just by our own vulnerabilities but also by the profound complexities of life.

Which brings me back to my favorite question. "What is the deepest longing of your heart?" I'm convinced that before we can feel cherished and before our lives can be full of meaning, we need to experience what it's like to be a leaf on the sea - ungrounded and desperate and blown about by the wind. The trauma exposes our need for something beyond ourselves and once we grab onto it, we become deep and compassionate and begin bearing fruit that would never have been possible otherwise.

It reminds me of a passage in the gospels where we are likened to branches on a vine. All the nourishment comes from the vine. The branches can bear no fruit without it. Once that spiritual truth is planted in our souls, we become transformed into something new. We are no longer leaves on a sea but rather, cities on a hill and beacons of hope in a darkened space. It happens because at some point in our lives, we failed and were willing to learn something significant. It seems to be the only way to satisfy that yearning in our souls - to be cherished deeply and to live a life full of meaning.

33

Mars Hill Revisited

I've been a debater all my life. My dad and I used to duke it out around the dinner table when I was a kid. We liked the competition and the challenge of new ideas. My best lessons in life came after losing debates. The most important of those lessons taught me that logic is rarely enough to change a person's heart. We don't realize this when we are young and foolish. We don't understand that rationality without love will almost always fail. But after many exasperating defeats, a question emerges in every maturing soul: How do I convince anyone of anything if logic is unpersuasive?

One of the great centers of debate in the ancient world was the city of Athens. The early Greeks loved wrestling with truths and falsehoods in the free marketplace of ideas. It was here that the word 'sophist' was first attributed to young scholars who were required to stand on street corners - arguing for one position in the morning and the opposite position in the afternoon. It was a way to fine-tune their debating skills and at the same time, figure out for themselves what they actually believed. The best persuaders were the ones who could find something in common with their audience so that they might be endeared to their listeners. These debaters understood that if people identified with them, they were more likely to prevail because the gift of persuasion relies on being lovable as much as being logical.

In 51 AD, a preacher from an obscure sect ascended Mars Hill in Athens to promote the idea of monotheism to a population of polytheists. He knew it was a sensitive topic. He knew he would upset the entire economy of the region by questioning their core beliefs. He could have been defined by a pompous arrogance but he chose a different way...

On his way to the debate, he noticed an altar with the inscription, "To an unknown god" so the first thing he did was to commend his listeners' agnosticism. In a way, we all have an unknown God. We understand that God is mysterious and often incomprehensible and that sometimes our journeys leave us groping in the dark. This preacher was well-acquainted with groping in the dark. He had once been defined by cruelty and pride. He had even presided over the execution of martyrs. But one day he was brought to his knees when he realized the depth of his own depravity. Now, several years later, he stood on Mars Hill before a crowd of skeptics and validated their willingness to acknowledge something important: There are truths hidden from us all that may still be discovered when scholarship and love meet.

To that preacher, love was greater than even faith or hope. Without it, we are all just clanging cymbals- unable to persuade anyone of anything.

I once heard about a rabbi who befriended a white

supremacist in prison. The angry young felon had never been loved. He had tattoos all over his body and rage in his soul but the rabbi kept returning to the prison to visit his troubled 'friend.' Eventually, the young prisoner found redemption. That rabbi was the only person who had ever loved him and as the young man began to embrace that love, his heart melted and his former hatreds disintegrated.

A little while ago, I read a personal testimony by a young Muslim woman who was living in Texas. She was in her 20s and had an infant. Her husband was abusive and she had to leave him and go into a homeless shelter. She had no money, no food, no car, no education. She called upon Allah to help her and she put her trust in him to protect and redeem her from her circumstances. Then things began happening. Someone offered her a car. Someone else gave her a part time job. Someone else showed her how to register at a local community college. As time progressed, all of her needs were met and she was grateful for God's goodness to her. As I read her testimony, I couldn't help thinking that it sounded just like a Christian testimony. That young Muslim woman was adored by her Maker.

Love means meeting people where they're at. It doesn't mean waiting for someone to measure up to some standard before it's offered. Love becomes incarnate when we pitch our tent beside a hurting soul and begin a tender relationship.

There's a story in the book of Genesis. It's the messy story of Abraham and Sarah and Hagar and Ishmael. When God first called Abraham, he knew Abraham was wandering aimlessly. Abraham hailed from Ur of the Chaldeans and everyone there believed in regional gods. Abraham is the father of three great faiths but he never read a single page of the Torah, Gospels, or Quran. He knew almost nothing about God. But according to Genesis, God met him where he was and they began a journey of faith together. God also met Hagar where she was - even after Abraham sent her away with Ishmael into the desert alone. Despite the messiness of their lives, all the characters in that story were loved by God and blessings were promised to each of them.

I believe all human beings have flawed theology. Our minds are finite and incapable of understanding the infinite. If perfect theology were demanded from Jews, Christians, Muslims, Hindus and Buddhists, we would all be in deep doo-doo. But the impossible isn't required of us. Our Lover only asks for a broken and contrite heart. His yoke is easy and his burden is light. He meets each of us exactly where we are and if we are willing to be persuaded by his love, we can begin a journey of faith that redeems us from our hatreds, ignorance and narcissism as we encounter the ineffable - something so sacred that it's not capable of being fully expressed or fully known. It is this ineffable character of God that keeps us humble as we look through a glass dimly - waiting for the day when we can see him face to face.

34

Keeping Vigil

When I was a boy growing up in the 1950s, I heard about a woman who lost her son during World War 2. His body was never found and even his dog tags were lost to history. The mother was unable to accept the tragedy. She wanted to believe that her son was still alive and that he had amnesia and that's why he hadn't come home. So each morning she sat by her front window and told herself that someday her son would come walking down the road and into her loving arms. She sat there day after day, week after week, month after month, and year after year. She essentially stopped living because the truth was too painful to bear.

We often think of truth in lofty terms. We equate it with enlightenment and learning, intellectual freedom and political liberation. We all claim to value it and desire it. But sometimes, truth isn't what we want.

There are some who say that we are now living in a 'Post-Truth Age.' It is an age where objective, verifiable facts are dismissed simply because they discomfort us or implicate us.

But if we distort the truth or deny it altogether, we become unteachable. Just because truth is unpleasant, doesn't make it any less true. In American society, it is becoming increasingly acceptable to define truth in any way that makes us happy but when we do, it loses all of its redemptive power.

And that's where the word "Integrity" enters the equation.

When I was raising kids, I used to tell them that integrity is the willingness to follow the truth wherever it leads – even if it leads to a painful place where we have to say, "I'm sorry. I was wrong. Would you forgive me? How can I make this right?"

I have several friends who are medical doctors. Some of them have spoken to me about what it's like to tell a patient that he has a life-threatening disease. Some patients get immediately angry. Some even assault their doctors. Others will get very pensive and not say a single word – seemingly overwhelmed by the news. Others will choose denial and accuse their doctor of stupidity.

But what about you? If you had cancer and didn't know it yet, would you want your doctor to tell you a pretty lie or the ugly truth? If he tells you the pretty lie and says "you're perfectly healthy," you can go home, lay your head on a pillow and have a deep restful sleep.

But your future is a funeral.

If your doctor tells you the ugly truth, he will also tell you your options. He will talk about chemo and radiation and he may describe the hell you might endure as you lose your hair, your strength and your dinners every night. But he will also tell you that you could beat this disease. If you're a fighter and you submit to someone more knowledgeable than yourself, and you allow the truth to penetrate your soul so that every effort is made to save your life, you have a chance of being victorious.

So what will it be? A pretty lie? Or the ugly truth? One will make you happy temporarily and then it will kill you. The other, though painful, might send you into remission so that you can have a full and joyful life.

One thing is certain, there can be no healing without a proper diagnosis and only the truth can transform our lives into something better than it is right now.

What is true for the human body, is also true for the body politic. Without truth and a population that embraces it, a nation cannot survive. It will simply begin its long descent into historical oblivion and its rejection of integrity will be its own demise.

I am frightened for my country right now. There are men in power who have no regard for facts. They call real news "fake" and fake news "real". They deny the abuse of the innocent. They demean women. They condemn a free press for asking difficult yet necessary questions. They are incapable of remorse or humility and exonerate themselves by blaming their victims. They mock sound science and belittle those who want the earth protected from mindless exploitation. They take away health insurance from the vulnerable. They claim to have the answers to all of our problems. They ask for our trust while their own lives are defined by infidelity to their wives and infidelity to the truth. Virtue is sacrificed on the altar of ignorance.

When people of faith dismiss the truth because it conflicts with their politics, they not only destroy their integrity, they destroy their witness as well. Someone once said, "*It takes a lifetime to create a good reputation. It only takes a few minutes to destroy it."*

When I was little, my dad had a habit of discovering my wayward behaviors. I would do something of dubious merit and he would find out about it and say, "The truth always outs." I think that phrase originated with Shakespeare. It basically means that no matter how hard we try to conceal the facts, they will eventually become known.

When I look back at my childhood and the impish things I did, it's easy to see why immaturity would try to conceal itself. After all, what little boy wants to tell a truth that implicates him? But as we move into adulthood, we realize that maturity means admitting our mistakes and acknowledging painful truths.

Truth can be beautiful or ugly. I heard a beautiful truth once when a midwife told me I was the father of a healthy baby boy. Years later, I heard an ugly truth when a sheriff informed me that an avalanche had taken my son's life.

It's easy to embrace beautiful truth. But ugly truth requires a level of maturity that can terrify our souls. The real test of our character isn't found in how we respond to beautiful truth. It is found in our ability to acknowledge ugly, painful truths that require us to grow.

Some people who seem very powerful are actually quite weak because they aren't able to acknowledge ugly truths or admit a failure. When Vladimir Putin realized that his war on Ukraine had turned into a debacle, he immediately shut down press freedom in Russia. He knew what would happen if his people learned the facts so he concealed the truth the way little boys do. Then he tried to make himself look righteous. He was 'killing nazis' so everything was justified. Displacing millions of innocent civilians, bombing hospitals, raping women, murdering children - it was all spun as a noble cause and anyone who questioned it was, in his mind, a traitor.

Richard Rohr once wrote, "*Evil is always incapable of critiquing itself. It depends upon disguise and tries to look like virtue."*

It would be tempting to conclude that we in the West are somehow morally superior to our Russian counterparts but the human condition transcends national boundaries. I've known sweet, loving Americans who chose to run away from difficult truths. The ugly persistence of racism, the deadliness of a virus, the violence of a fool-filled insurrection and a looming climate disaster are just a few such truths. Sometimes a person can be in such a state of denial that a lie, like some tempting intoxicant, becomes irresistible. It is especially difficult to witness this in a loved one. It's like watching a person's conscience evaporate from his soul.

Václav Havel, the famous Czech writer once wrote, *"Hope is not the conviction that something will turn out well, but the certainty that something is worth doing no matter how it turns out."*[26]

Speaking truth is worth doing. Even if the truth is ugly. Even if it slams us to the floor. Even if it demands that we rethink every priority we've ever had because without truth, redemption isn't possible. The alternative is a deadened conscience and a destroyed reputation. This is why it's so important for us to keep vigil over our own souls. Self-deception comes easy to the human race despite the fact that there is no

---

[26] Vaclav Havel, Disturbing the Peace (New York: Vintage Books, 1991)

lasting comfort in the lies we tell.

As an artist, I'm sometimes asked to sculpt a human face. When I first rough-in the basic contours of the nose and cheek bones I can easily get discouraged because the face goes through an ugly phase. I haven't yet removed enough material for the sculpture to look right. It isn't until the very end of the process that I begin to feel proud of my work. A lot of waste has to be removed first. It's time-consuming and messy but I keep telling myself, it will be beautiful when I'm finished.

When truth 'outs', something similar takes place. It's like a hammer and a chisel in the hands of a sculptor who longs to remove all the falsehoods that disfigure our lives. Painful truth can reshape our character and make us beautiful. It has the power to chip away at our stone facades until the real person beneath our fear begins to take shape. This is the only way to become truly known and deeply LOVED. The process might be accompanied by pain but it's also merciful because it invites us into a new life where we finally become the person we were always meant to be. When we are tempted to find comfort in a lie, truth says, "Don't. Don't harden your heart. Don't enslave your soul. Trust the process. It's messy. It's time-consuming. But you were meant to be beautiful."

Michelangelo once said, *"I saw the angel in the marble and carved until I set her free."*

35

The Rude Vigor of Truth

When I was young, my dad used to call me "Michelangelo." I earned that nickname after a hornet chased me off a high ladder while I was painting the house. My gallon of paint took flight in a fanciful sort of way before landing in the neighbor's yard and I fell two stories into a pricker bush. The resulting masterpiece on the lawn next door looked like a Jackson Pollock painting but my dad preferred to name me after a Renaissance man.

It's funny how a cranky hornet or a nickname like "Michelangelo" can cause a kid to wonder about his calling in life, but that's what happened. I knew I wasn't an artistic genius but when I was a teenager, Michelangelo and his buddies in the Renaissance fascinated me. The Great Masters excelled in so many disciplines because they were never satisfied and they constantly pushed the envelope beyond society's expectations. So I decided that I wanted to push the envelope too. I started asking, "Why?" about all kinds of things and rarely avoided the trouble that inquisitive minds encounter in stale, stagnant places. About the same time my dad and I would get into friendly debates about politics and theology which always upset my mom because she didn't think they were friendly at all.

Then I noticed something. While the heroes of the Renaissance were integrating faith and art, they were also questioning themselves. It's the nature of true genius to grapple with one's own subjectivity and to see it as an obstacle to a person's quest for truth. The Renaissance produced thinkers who weren't afraid to challenge themselves and they even seemed to frolic through the task. I wanted to do that. I wanted to be suspicious of myself and my motives. I wanted to poke holes in my own theories in order to become better than I was ...and I wanted to have fun doing it. Maybe this is because the only way to really study anything is with a mischievous glint in our eyes. So I decided to study law, theology, literature, history, art, and legos with an impish devotion. Legos were my favorite. Give me a few rowdy kids and a giant box of legos and our grand unifying theory will bring order to any chaos. Over the years I've learned that the only way to understand complex stuff is to have the mind of a child. Old brains are often calcified. New brains are inquisitive and pliable and open to new perspectives.

Which brings me to the subject I really want to talk about. Perspective determines everything. It can destroy a relationship or mend one. It can cause us to stagnate or it can enable growth. It can divide us into clusters of parochial misfits, or it can heal a nation.

The other day I saw a comment on a friend's Facebook page. It was on the topic of abortion and, as we all know, few subjects are more fraught with raw emotion than that one. It's not my intention to write about abortion here. I just want to talk about perspective and our need to always question the one we have. The comment I saw accused someone of "killing babies at full term" as if the person was completely unaware of the painful medical realities that accompany rare, late term abortions. The person who made the comment will probably never know the heartbreak that expecting parents feel when something has gone terribly wrong with a pregnancy and a child cannot survive outside of the womb. Instead, that person will stay in her protective cloister, comforted by the pretense of her own moral superiority and refuse to see life in anything other than black and white terms.

It made me realize something: When we're in a rut, we often don't know we're in a rut and the only way to get out of the rut is to listen carefully to other perspectives. I know there are brilliant people in both camps so obviously the problem isn't a lack of intelligence. But if we divide into our own comfortable subcultures where the only information we hear affirms us rather than challenges us, all of our intelligence goes to waste.

Extremists like to congregate in closed systems. They know that if they ever mingled with other people, they might learn uncomfortable things. So they stay isolated and never mature into thoughtful adults who are capable of processing the complexities of life. I spent years in one of those closed systems. It was a nurturing faith community but it also had a bad habit of withdrawing from the rest of society for fear of being tainted. The result was a fear-based system that destroyed scholastic integrity. Os Guinness described those who embrace such systems when he wrote, "Retreating into the fortress of personal experience, they can pull up the drawbridge of faith and feel impregnable to reason. But ...the outcome is a sickly faith deprived of the rude vigor of truth."

The thing is, when we stay in closed systems, we tend to define truth with our emotions rather than facts. But no matter how badly we might want something to be true, it doesn't make it true. So we need to ask ourselves, "What do we want more? To be blissfully unaware of life's disturbing complexities? ...or to be defined by integrity?" Another useful question might be: "How long can we hold onto our falsehoods before they completely destroy us?"

If we were brutally honest with ourselves we would have to admit that nobody really believes in an absolute right to privacy or an absolute right to life. If a young child is being molested, few liberals would object to a police officer invading the privacy of a bedroom to protect that child. Why? Because a child is more important than the privacy of a molester. Similarly, few American conservatives have ever objected to the incineration of innocent women and children in order to end a war sooner (Hiroshima and Nagasaki). They might howl against 'moral relativism' in their churches but they are actually its greatest proponents.

I usually try to write comforting things for people who are hurt but honestly, healing only happens after we acknowledge a problem. If we want to be defined by integrity, it's important to realize that we are all myopic and the only way to transcend our blinding biases is to question ourselves and test our own theories and listen humbly to an opposing view and resist the temptation to demonize others. Life is rarely tidy and some things aren't black and white. Truth is always more complicated than extremists want us to believe and if we can't understand that, we will never be able to dispense grace to another hurting soul.

36

Shaking the Dust

Have you ever tried to help someone who didn't want to be helped? ...or teach someone who didn't want to be taught? ...or free someone who was happily trapped in their own echo chamber? I used to feel obligated to engage in such endeavors even though beating my head against a brick wall would probably have been more enjoyable. Then I stumbled upon some wisdom. Before I tell you about it, I'd like to share a happy story...

Several summers ago I was driving down a Vermont country road when I spotted a young woman walking by herself. It seemed unusual to me because there were no homes or businesses in the immediate area and I knew she had a long way to walk. She was also black (Vermont is the whitest state in the country) and she looked a bit dejected.

So after passing her, I put on my brakes and backed up down the road until I was beside her and then I asked, "Would you like a ride?"

She thanked me with a Jamaican accent and climbed into

my car. We began to exchange stories about ourselves. Her name was Shanique and she grew up on a farm in the central part of her country. She saw the cycle of poverty and despair and she saw young women getting pregnant and being abandoned. She determined that she wasn't going to be part of it and decided that an education was the only way out of her circumstances. One day she got a ride to Kingston and walked into the admissions office at the University of the West Indies. She told the receptionist that she needed to go to school but she had no money. The receptionist said, "I'm sorry. We can't help you."

Shanique wouldn't give up. She just sat down in that office and said, "I must go to school." She was very persistent. When we talked, I could see that she had a fire in her soul and seemed more determined than anyone I've met. Finally, after waiting hours in that office, she noticed that the receptionist got up, left the room, and apparently told a supervisor that there was a young woman in the next room who wasn't going to take "no" for an answer. A few minutes later, Shanique was enrolled in college.

She graduated with her Bachelor's degree four years later. When I met her, she was 25 years old and working towards a Master's degree in government and public policy. She also had a loving heart for powerless people. When I told her about losing my son and visiting Nicaragua and adopting Jenny, she said, "God bless you" and we began to exchange our journeys of faith.

Before dropping her off at her destination that day, I asked, "How do you get your groceries without a car?" She didn't answer. She just looked sad. So I wrote my phone number on a piece of paper and said, "I'm not available in the mornings but I can drive you wherever you need to go in the afternoons." She thanked me and said goodbye.

That night I received a Facebook message from her. She told me that she had been walking that road all summer long and no one had ever offered her a ride. When I picked her up she was at an all-time low. She had borrowed money to come to the U.S. so she could earn income by cleaning hotel rooms and making beds but business was slow and she wasn't earning the money she needed to finish her schooling. She took a second job at a small country store near me but on some days, she would walk two hours and be given only an hour of work. She had holes in her shoes and blisters on her toes and feet and she was emotionally exhausted.

The next day I took her grocery shopping and bought her some new shoes and we made sure that she had the funds she needed for school. I spent the next few weeks meeting with her. We had several meals together. I love listening to people from other cultures. I love hearing how their obstacles and trials deepen their characters and their faith. I love seeing their joy when they are treated with dignity.

Shanique just completed her Master's degree. We talk everyday online and she has become one of my dearest friends. I keep being reminded over and over again that the most beautiful people in the world are those who have suffered. They have more to give us than we could ever give them. Which brings me back to the wisdom I stumbled upon after wasting years trying to teach the unteachable...

There's a story in the gospels that I had seen many times before. It describes the first time that Jesus sent out his disciples into the countryside. He was going to stay behind and not accompany them. Before he sent them he said, *"Look! The fields are white with harvest!"* In other words, there are literally thousands of people who are dying to hear the good news that they are valued and adored by the Lover of their souls. Then Jesus said, *"If you come to a house that won't receive you, just chill. It's ok. Shake the dust from your feet and move on. Why? Because, Look! The fields are white with harvest!"* (Will's Paraphrased Version).

Although I had read that passage before, this was the first time it grabbed me. I found myself saying, "Do you see how wasteful you've been? You've spent so many years of your life in houses that wouldn't receive you - even when the fields were ready for harvest. Instead of being cranky and unfulfilled, you could have been having fun. Instead of accomplishing nothing, you could have been doing something significant."

If you are a little cranky about living an unfulfilling life, I would suggest that the fields are still white with harvest. There are still thousands of people who would love for us to dignify them and empower them so that they can live meaningful lives. We can find them in our own communities with blisters on their toes and feet – wishing that someone would love them.

37

Unseen Things

When my dad was in art school, he was taught how to see. It was always fascinating to hear him talk about things that were right in front of our faces but were unnoticed by us. My dad would comment on the shadow cast by a person's nose or the highlight on moist lips or the shape of an earlobe. He was trained to observe these things because a painter has to put everything he sees onto canvas.

Things like truth and spiritual beauty can also exist in our world without ever being noticed by us. They can be right in front of our faces but we haven't been trained to see them. Sometimes we are even trained NOT to see them. Sometimes our culture blinds us.

For instance, the affluence and ease of the American experience can cause us to not notice things that are readily seen in Developing Countries. This is especially true in matters of faith. Those who have suffered the indignities of injustice notice all the verses in scripture that speak to that subject while those who are comfortable aren't even interested in them.

Before I say more, I should tell you about Corn Flakes. I know it's just cereal, but it's also a perfect metaphor for something beautiful. A few years ago, the Kellogg Company wanted to advertise their cereal on TV but they knew the usual marketing techniques wouldn't work. They couldn't tell us their flakes were new and improved because they weren't. They were the same old flakes that had been around since the 1800s. There was another problem too. Corn Flakes was facing stiff competition from a lot of new-fangled cereals with fruits and nuts and crunchy things. How does a company compete against THAT - especially when the two best adjectives for Corn Flakes are "corny" and "flakey?" But still, people like the simple, good old-fashioned taste of the stuff.

So one day, an advertising genius came up with a slogan that went like this: "Corn Flakes: Taste them again for the first time."

It was the kind of slogan that makes us think. How can we taste them *again* if it's the first time? And then we'd get the point. Sometimes something good can be right in front of our faces for decades and we don't notice it or we forget about it or we take it for granted or we are distracted by other things or we belong to a group that doesn't want us to see...

There is a phrase used in American politics these days that always generates a lot of heated debate. The phrase is 'class warfare.' Very often that phrase is used to defend a certain economic theory which claims that poor people are lazy and unmotivated while rich people are hardworking and industrious. The theory argues that we shouldn't punish the wealthy with taxes and we shouldn't encourage laziness with social programs because such things are disincentives to productivity and anyone who argues otherwise is engaging in class warfare.

I would like to show you some of the most extreme examples of class warfare I've ever found. They are the kinds of words that would ordinarily alarm us all except for the very awkward fact that they come from the Bible itself. Here they are. Taste them again for the first time...

> "My soul magnifies the Lord,
> And my spirit rejoices in God my Savior,
> ...He has scattered the proud in the imagination of their hearts,
> He has put down the mighty from their thrones,
> And exalted those of low degree;
> He has filled the hungry with good things,
> and the rich he has sent away empty-handed."[27]

> "The Lord has entered into judgment
> With the elders and princes of his people;
> 'It is you who have devoured the vineyard,
> The spoil of the poor is in your houses,
> What do you mean by crushing my people,
> By grinding the face of the poor?'"[28]

> "You say, 'I am rich, I have prospered, and I need nothing'; not knowing that you are wretched, pitiable, poor, blind, and naked."[29]

---

[27] Luke 1:31-33
[28] Isaiah 3:14,15
[29] Revelation 3:17

"Come now, you rich, weep and howl for the miseries coming upon you. Behold, the wages of the laborers who mowed your fields which you kept back by fraud, cry out and the cries of the harvesters have reached the ears of God Almighty. You have lived on the earth in luxury and self-indulgence; you have fattened your hearts in a day of slaughter. You have condemned and killed the innocent man."[30]

*"Blessed are you who are poor,
For yours is the Kingdom of God.
Blessed are you who hunger now,
For you will be satisfied.
But woe to you who are rich,
for you have already received your comfort."*[31]

*"For wicked men are found among my people;
They lurk like fowlers lying in wait,
They set a trap to catch men.
Like a basket full of birds,
Their houses are full of treachery;
Therefore they have become great and rich,
They have grown fat and sleek.
They do not judge with justice the cause of the fatherless
They do not defend the rights of the poor."*[32]

---

30 James 5:1-6
31 Luke 20,24
32 Jeremiah 5-26-28

*"Hear this, you who trample upon the needy,
And bring the poor of the land to an end:
Surely I will not forget any of your deeds.
Shall not the land tremble on this account,
and everyone mourn who dwells in it?"*[33]

*"Is this not the faithfulness I choose:
To loose the bonds of wickedness,
To undo the thongs of slavery,
To let the oppressed go free,
And to shatter every form of exploitation?*

*If you pour yourself out for the hungry
And satisfy the desires of the afflicted,
Then shall your light rise in the darkness
And your gloom become like the noonday sun."*[34]

*"He has shown you O man, what is good;
And what does the Lord require of you
But to do justice, and to love kindness,
and to walk humbly with your God?"*[35]

There are literally hundreds of verses like these in the Bible. They raise a few inescapable questions: What do they say about the character of God? What do they say about the character of those who preach the authority of scripture while ignoring any parts of it that conflict with their political

---

[33] Amos 8:4,8
[34] Isaiah 58:6,7,10
[35] Micah 6-8

agenda? What has to take place in our hearts before our eyes can see what has been right in front of our faces all along? Isaiah, Jeremiah, Micah, Luke, John, James, Jesus. *Taste them again for the first time...*

38

Grace and Power

Sometimes I think odd things. I've got these ideas about what leadership should look like and who should be in positions of authority, but my ideas don't fit most of the models I've seen. I think the best leaders are reluctant ones. They are people who don't crave attention and they tend to shy away from the limelight. I love people like that because their egos don't get in the way and they delight in seeing others succeed.

Over the years, I've become convinced that if leadership is done right, it's almost always invisible. A true leader doesn't hoard power. He doesn't cultivate a cult of personality. He doesn't strut a stage like a night club performer. He (or she) empowers gifted people to do what they're gifted to do so that everyone can experience the joy of being valued and fruitful. This is what happens when organizations really shine. A true leader finds joy in lifting others up. She doesn't need a spotlight on her. She prefers to shine that light on others. If a leader craves attention, he wants leadership for the wrong reasons. A poor leader isn't interested in serving others. He's interested in being served. I once read an anonymous quote that said, *"If servanthood is beneath you, leadership is beyond you."*

There's a reason why this idea of a "servant-leader" is so beautiful. I don't think we can ever lead well until we've experienced the pain of powerlessness or the shame of being vulnerable. True leaders learn humility and compassion in the crucible of trauma. Once they've survived those experiences, their hearts begin to melt when they see other hurting people. Their grief awakens in them the very best attributes of a leader. This is why I've never been impressed by "born leaders." Very often such people possess a presumptuous confidence that looks and feels like narcissism.

Loving leaders are actually grateful for their weaknesses because their sense of vulnerability drives them to their knees and compels them to look for something beyond themselves. As a result, they are able to accomplish so much more than if they relied solely on their own abilities. It is in that state of brokenness and humility that real transformation occurs. *"My grace is sufficient for you, for my power is made perfect in weakness."*[36]

A few months ago I found a photo of mating egrets. It illustrated something beautiful about power and grace and how both attributes must be present before leadership can be authentic. The two birds are engaged in a courtship. Both are powerful. Both are graceful. Each one's success is determined by the other. Even when one partner leads, it's difficult to discern because each one's beauty brings glory to the other.

A failing leader on the other hand thinks he doesn't need

---

[36] 2 Corinthians 12:9

anyone. He says, "I'm the only one who matters." "I alone can fix your problems." "Nobody matters but me." People look away in disgust when they see such arrogance. It repulses anyone who desires decency.

I am sorry to say that some of the worst examples of leadership I've witnessed were found in churches. I once experienced a church that so tightly controlled the flow of information, that everyone was hesitant to speak. The minister had a habit of mistaking his opinions for God's and anyone who suggested otherwise was accused of rebelliousness. When his insecurities defined him, they undermined the church's scholastic integrity. Needless to say, I didn't last long there. I remember the minister was often concerned that I might say something inappropriate if I spoke publicly. One time I spoke anyway and I could see him shifting nervously in his seat like one of those actors in a Preparation-H commercial. It was unnerving.

That experience taught me that fear-based leadership denigrates people but love-based leadership lifts people up. Bad leaders want respect but they don't know how to earn it. I think this is because there are two kinds of "respect" and poor leaders aren't able to appreciate the difference. The first kind of respect is the kind we have for a loaded gun. We know not to look down its barrel because something violent and unpredictable might happen. The second kind of respect is the kind shown by two lovers whose romance has survived the test of time. It is a respect based on the tenderness and predictability of the loving character. It's easy to earn the first kind of respect. One only has to be a self-centered jerk. Earning the second kind of respect requires a willingness to live a sacrificial life.

On one of my trips to Latin America, I saw some artwork done by an eleven year old girl living in a garbage dump. Her talent amazed me. It also made me sad. I began to ask God, "Why do you give people talents if they are trapped in poverty with little opportunity to use those talents because each day is a struggle merely to survive?"

...and then I realized something about the nature of servant leadership. I think God longs to whisper something redemptive into each of our souls. I think he wants to say, "My job is to give people talents. Your job is to empower them to use those talents. If I did everything, you would have no mission. If you have no mission, your life loses meaning. If your life loses meaning, you will have no joy. I promised you joy. I promised you an abundant life. This is how you get it. Feed my lambs. Love the brokenhearted. Empower the powerless. Don't do it for your own glory. Do it for something bigger than you."

When God weeps such words onto the pages of our souls, we are brought to our knees by the beauty of it all. It transports us to a place of healing where we no longer have any interest in our own vain glory, because now (finally), our lives are defined by depth, maturity, significance and joy..

39

Making Joy

When I was a little boy, I would sometimes say to my mom, "I'm bored." She would always respond by smiling mischievously and saying, "Take off your sock and spit in your shoe." It was a nonsensical comment but we both knew what it meant. It was my mom's way of saying, "No one is responsible for your happiness except you. Happiness is something that begins inside us. If you are bored or exasperated or unhappy, there is a way to fix it and the responsibility is yours."

Years later a counselor taught me the difference between an emotionally secure person and someone who is emotionally insecure. She said when insecure people are sad, they will service an addiction, find a new lover, get a new job or buy a lot of stuff. They will change the externals without ever examining the true source of their unhappiness. An emotionally secure person will ask, "What do I need to change inside myself in order to find joy again?"

It takes courage to ask that question but if we don't examine ourselves honestly, we can't grow. Tolstoy once wrote,

"Everyone thinks of changing the world but no one thinks of changing himself."

It seems so much easier to make other people responsible for our happiness but one day I realized that I would much rather be in charge of my own destiny than give that responsibility to people who might not even love me.

Sometimes our unhappiness really *is* due to external events but the principle still remains. There are things we can do inside ourselves that can alter the trajectory of our lives and fill us with joy. During my darkest days I would often tell myself, "There is still joy to be found." Two dead kids and an unfaithful wife didn't mean I had to be sad forever.

Sometimes joy comes wrapped in unexpected packages. Other times it might require a leap of faith with a beautiful surprise at the end. As I thought about what I needed to change within me, I discovered a strange paradox. If my life was to be filled with meaning, my focus couldn't be solely on my needs, my grief, my history. I know that sounds counterintuitive but here's a little story…

A few years ago, I met a young woman who was struggling economically. I was impressed by her determination and the way she held herself with dignity. We met in Vermont but she was about to return to her native country. Before she left, she said, "I can't believe how FREE I am here." I asked her what she meant. She replied, I can walk anywhere without being robbed or beaten or raped."

We stayed in touch after she returned home and the more I learned about her struggles, the more I cherished her. She would tell me how she would spend three to four hours each day waiting for buses and taxis to take her to work and back.

It was not a safe situation. The threat of violence was always present. Sometimes thieves would pose as taxi drivers and rob passengers at gun point. There was so much poverty and desperation in that culture that no one could ever feel safe. One morning, my friend woke up to the sound of a woman crying beside her house. When she went outside to look, she found the dead body of the taxi driver who had brought her home the night before. He had been brutally murdered. She told me, "Will, I wish I never looked. I can't get the image out of my mind."

By this time, I was genuinely terrified for my friend. She had just acquired a decent job so I gave her the down payment for a car. That one act changed everything for her. It also changed the lives of everyone in her family. Now, they could be so much more efficient with their time because they no longer had to stand on unsafe street corners waiting for buses and taxis. They could go grocery shopping and to the doctor without fearing for their lives.

After a little while I realized something. I lost my family but I found my purpose by being engaged in the lives of vulnerable people. I removed people from my life who diminished me and I embraced people who valued me. It brought so much more depth and meaning to my life. I changed my focus and became a happy person who could finally say, "I know who I am and I know why I'm here."

We aren't all called to the same purpose. We each have different gifts and talents but the principle is the same. Discovering our true purpose can lead to a reorienting of priorities and overwhelming joy soon follows. I love encouraging people and I believe that nobody is a nobody. I'm also convinced that joy isn't just something that we stumble upon. It is something we can actively create. The alternative is to obsess about our losses or disappointments and fall deeper and deeper into despair.

Eleanor Roosevelt once said some wise words: *"Happiness isn't a goal. It is a byproduct of a life well lived."*

40
Rising from the Dead

Have you ever wondered whether words might be living things? Maybe only crazy writers think that way. For many years, I assumed I knew what words were - only because I saw them everywhere. I thought they were just inanimate things made of vowels and consonants. But when I viewed them that way and put them together, nothing magical ever happened. I could form correct sentences. But they didn't inspire anyone. Sentences can seem lifeless when a writer shows no tenderness to his words. Maybe words are like people. We shouldn't use them. We should love them.

So now I've come to realize that words are like spiritual beings that want intimacy with us. When we meet them in a place of mystery, and see them as mystical creatures - begging to be known, they reward us with wonders. I think the best writing happens when we relate to words this way. A word is like a woman who wants to be cherished. She will reveal her deepest secrets to me if she sees I'm safe and I won't take her for granted. Often when I write, it feels like a muse is showing me things that

I'm not able to understand without her. When she comes to me at night and asks for my undivided attention, she might offer a single word - one attribute of her soul - and then she will unwrap it like a present. It's amazing what a word can really mean when I bare myself and delve inside her. There's one word in particular that I make love to all the time. She is the one who means the most to me. She's tender and passionate and she whispers comforting thoughts even though she's sad. Everything of consequence that I've ever written has been inspired by her. She can also mean opposite things so I have to be careful to approach her with understanding. Her name, is 'broken.'

There are two kinds of 'broken.' One disallows intimacy, while the other pleads for it. There is 'broken beyond repair' (which I associate with narcissism and spiritual death) and there is 'broken and contrite' (which is the beginning of life and everything good). I want to talk about that second kind of 'broken' because she is the one who has caressed her meaning into my soul. She is the one who always visits me at night when no one else is near. She is the one I have fallen hopelessly in love with.

But first, a little story...

When I was a kid, I think I had ADD. It was in the olden days before educators even made such assessments. But I got bored easily and didn't focus very well on my schoolwork. If I wasn't being stimulated, I would just retreat into my own little world. When my parents brought me to church, the monotony and predictability of it made me want to cry. It was a liturgical church where a lot of 400 year old Germanic dirges were sung and I remember wanting to tear certain songs out of the hymnals so we wouldn't have to sing them anymore. Every Sunday when we got home from church, my mom would make a scrumptious dinner and we'd sometimes talk about spiritual things. One day my parents turned to my siblings and me and said, "Why don't you invite your friends to church next week?" I think I was only 7 years old but I remember saying, "If they are my friends, why would I do that to them?" My parents always seemed puzzled when I said such things but really, I was the one who was puzzled. Throughout my entire childhood I had been told that the Creator of the universe loved me deeply and wanted a relationship with me. I would often think, "If this is true, it's an amazing thing. So... why is church so boring? Why would something so beautiful be cloaked in something so stale and lifeless?"

When I got older, I learned some things. Even after reading Hegel and Marx I realized that the most scathing critique of religion I had ever found was in the pages of the Bible. It might surprise some of my readers but the idea that religion is an "opiate of the people" was first suggested by Jeremiah, Isaiah, and Jesus - long before the Secular Enlightenment. There is something about repeating the same old creeds and confessions over and over again that can lull a person to sleep and cause him to lose sight of everything that truly matters. Abraham Joshua Heschel once wrote,

> "When faith is replaced by creed, worship by discipline, love by habit; ...when faith becomes an heirloom rather than a living fountain... when religion speaks only in the name of authority rather than with the voice of compassion - its message becomes meaningless."[37]

---

37 Abraham Joshua Heschel, *God In Search of Man: A Philosophy of Judaism* (New York: Farrar, Straus and Giroux, 1976)

The fountain that Heschel spoke of was first mentioned in the book of Jeremiah:

> "Be appalled, O heavens, at this; be shocked, be utterly desolate, ...for my people have forsaken me, the fountain of living waters, and hewed out cisterns for themselves, broken cisterns that can hold no water."[38]

Those broken cisterns were the outward forms of religion - devoid of any deep, transformative power. At one point, Jeremiah described God as a heartbroken lover who had been forsaken and replaced by cold, lifeless orthodoxy. It's sad that religion can be synonymous with both idolatry and death.

Jesus once confronted the fundamentalists of his day - people who had a high view of scripture and who adhered to it with a brutal rigidity. He told them, *"Go and learn what this means, 'I desire mercy, not rituals.'"*[39] He claimed that those who placed unbearable burdens on the victims of their dogma were like "white-washed tombs filled with dead men's bones." Then Jesus turned to the crowds who only wanted to be loved and said,

> "Come unto me all you who labor and are heavy laden and I will give you rest."[40]

The thing is, we know when we're hungry. We know when our thirst isn't being quenched. 'There is a balm in Gilead' but

---

38 Jeremiah 2:12-13
39 Matthew 9:13
40 Matthew 11:28

it isn't found in broken cisterns.

...which brings me back to living words that speak to us in the middle of the night when no one else is near. Perhaps the muse isn't really a muse. Perhaps she is the Spirit of a tender God being introduced to us by a creature named 'broken'. I have come to know 'broken' intimately. She is full of mercy and she whispers comforting thoughts to anyone who will listen. She always waits until we cherish her - because words are like people. We shouldn't use them. We should only love them. 'Broken' knows that nothing meaningful will ever be ours without humility so when we're ready to give up our silly pretense of perfection, she will offer to remove the garments of our shame and clothe us in something better. She wants us to know, more than anything else, that there is a sorrow that leads to cynicism and a sorrow that leads to hope and that if we make the right choice, we won't have to be empty forever.

Such thoughts make me wonder about other things as well... What if there is a place of mystery that we can go to where a word isn't a cold, dead thing but a Spirit full of life? What if that Spirit is like a lover who cherishes us? ...or a physician who longs to heal our deepest wounds? ...or a Redeemer who emptied himself of everything so we could be filled? What if we could collapse into the arms of someone who is still saying, *"Come unto me and I will give you rest?"* What if awe is better than ritual? What if even now we could rise from the dead - into a life that is free from brittle religious formulas? What if compassion matters more than dogma? What if people who live in darkness could see a great light? What if that light is so brilliant and so beautiful that the darkness could never overcome it? What if this Living Word became flesh and dwelled among us and if we go to that place of mystery, with a broken and contrite heart, we can still behold the glory of it all?